Quick & Easy
Simple Indian

p

Contents

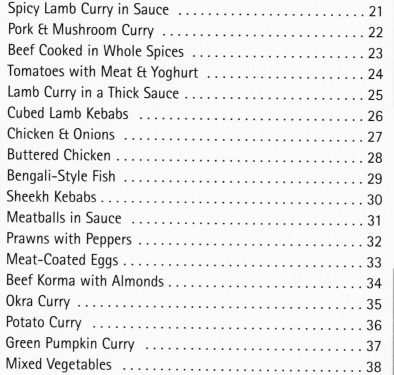

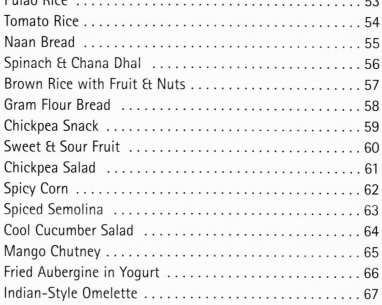

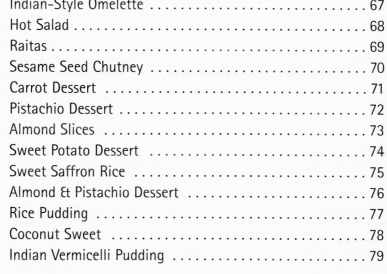

Introduction

Indian cuisine offers some of the most exciting and flavoursome food in the world. With around 900 million inhabitants living on more than 4 million square kilometres of land, it is not surprising that there is such a huge diversity of food with something to suit every taste. Dishes also vary according to the predominant religious influence in a given area: followers of the Muslim faith do not eat pork or any of its derivatives and similarly, Hindus do not eat beef as cows are considered to be sacred animals. In fact many traditional dishes are vegetarian and based on produce that can be grown locally. The meat-free dishes incorporate ingredients such as lentils and chickpeas to provide a balanced and nutritious diet. The sauces and side dishes are aromatic and colourful, each bringing a little bit of the Orient to your home.

Indian cookery is extremely easy. Many dishes can be prepared in advance and will usually keep in a refrigerator for a day or two. Generally curries are ideal for freezing and often improve on reheating as warming slowly over a low heat allows all the spices to release

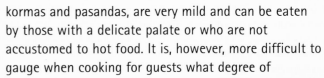

their flavours to be subsequently absorbed by the other ingredients.

It is important to read the recipes carefully before you begin cooking an Indian meal, as many of the dishes benefit from early preparation. The different dishes themselves are easy to make and many are very quick to cook, but some ingredients may require soaking or pre-cooking whilst others may need marinating overnight.

Hot and Spicy

For thousands of years India has been using a rich variety of herbs and spices in its cooking; it was from India that many important spices were introduced to the West. In attempts to defend the precious spice routes, Western nations fought in many wars, invested heavily in setting up transport networks and undertook dangerous voyages. Nowadays spices are ubiquitous and

cheap, except the costly saffron.

However, it is a myth that all Indian food is extremely hot and spicy. Many of the curries, such as

kormas and pasandas, are very mild and can be eaten by those with a delicate palate or who are not accustomed to hot food. It is, however, more difficult to gauge when cooking for guests what degree of spiciness is suitable. This depends on the amount of chilli, in whatever form — fresh, dry or ground — you add to the dish. It is recommended that you under- rather than over-estimate the amount of chilli you will need. In order to do this, remove the seeds from fresh chillies. Remember, authentic curries have a lot of flavour but not always a lot of 'heat'. Traditionally, Indian cooking combines a variety

of curries so that hotter dishes are served with cooler ones which may be yoghurt based.

Buying Spices

Whether you should buy spices ground or whole depends upon the quantity you will use. If you use one spice frequently then it may be better to buy this ground in a larger amount to save time. The more often you use spices, the more you will learn about how long their flavour and colour lasts. Black pepper, for example, keeps its essential oils reasonably well so you can afford to buy it in greater quantities. Those spices which you do not use often should be purchased whole as they will lose their aroma quickly when ground. In general, it is best to grind spices yourself. This can be done using a pestle and mortar or a coffee grinder. Spices should

be stored in air-tight containers away from direct heat and light. Jars should be washed and dried before adding newly bought spices so they are not mixed with an older purchase.

The amount of spices used can vary from two to 12 depending on the dish. However, some herbs and spices are particularly favoured in Indian gastronomy. Some of the most popular and important ingredients are described below.

Cardamom: This traditional Indian spice is delicious in curries. Cardamom must be purchased whole in its pod, which should be pale green, cream or dark brown and hairy. The seeds can be ground when you need them but they quickly lose their flavour.

Chana dhal: Similar to small, yellow split peas, this is used as a binding agent in Indian cooking.

Chickpeas: These hard golden peas have a wonderfully rich nutty flavour and are excellent in casserole-type dishes and curries. Canned chickpeas do not need soaking; the dried variety should be soaked for 5–8 hours.

Cinnamon sticks: The sticks are made from the dried, rolled bark of a tropical evergreen tree native to India.

Cinnamon sticks are particularly good for flavouring stews, but are difficult to grind so use powdered cinnamon for desserts.

Cumin seeds: This small, ridged seed gives a distinct, medium hot, sweetish flavour to food. Cumin seeds are extremely versatile and can be used with a variety of other spices.

Curry powder: Curry powders vary according to different cooks, regions or customs. A standard curry powder will contain turmeric, coriander (cilantro), cumin, pepper, cloves, cardamom, ginger, nutmeg, tamarind and chilli pepper, in varying amounts. Depending on the relative proportions of each of these spices, the powder is then classified as being either mild, hot or very hot.

Fenugreek seeds: These small, tan-coloured seeds are extremely important in Indian cooking. They are often used to make up mixed spices and some curry powders. The seeds must be lightly roasted before grinding.

Garam masala: This intensely aromatic mixture of ground spices is extremely popular in Indian cooking. Ready mixed, all-purpose garam masala contains cumin, coriander (cilantro), cardamom and black pepper. Unlike curry powder, garam masala should be added towards the end of cooking, and can be sprinkled on to the finished dish as a seasoning.

Ghee: Traditionally a form of clarified butter, it is made from gently heating butter until all the water has evaporated and the milk solids have sunk to the bottom. The remaining fat can cook at high temperatures without burning.

Ginger: One of the first spices to be used in the West, ginger is now widely available. Its flavour is hot and spicy yet refreshing. When buying ginger choose a smooth and plump-looking root. Store in the refrigerator with the peel on wrapped in clingfilm (plastic wrap) for up to six weeks.

Tamarind: The pulp from the pods of a tropical tree, it is generally sold dried or as a paste. Tamarind is dark brown with a refreshing acidic taste and is usually soaked in hot water before use. The sour liquid is then added to curries and chutneys.

Turmeric: Fresh turmeric root is similar to ginger but has a bright orange flesh. When dried and ground it produces a familiar yellow powder. Although it has a similar colour to saffron the taste is different. It lends a warm spicy flavour to dishes.

KEY

 Simplicity level 1 – 3 (1 easiest, 3 slightly harder)

 Preparation time

 Cooking time

Chicken Korma

Chicken korma is one of the most popular curries, and this one is perfect for a dinner party.

12.5 points

NUTRITIONAL INFORMATION

Calories 764   Protein 49g
Carbohydrate . . .24g   Sugars 8g
Fat . . . . .54g   Saturates 6g

🕒 15 MINS   🕐 40 MINS

SERVES 6

INGREDIENTS

1½ tsp fresh ginger root, finely chopped

1½ tsp fresh garlic, crushed

2 tsp garam masala

1 tsp chilli powder

1 tsp salt

1 tsp black cumin seeds

3 green cardamoms, with husks removed and seeds crushed

1 tsp ground coriander

1 tsp ground almonds

150 ml/5 fl oz/⅔ cup natural yogurt

6 whole chicken breasts, skinned

300 ml/½ pint/1¼ cups oil

2 medium onions, sliced

150 ml/½ pint/⅔ cup water

fresh coriander (cilantro) leaves

green chillies, chopped

boiled rice, to serve

1 Mix the ginger, garlic, garam masala, chilli powder, salt, black cumin seeds, green cardamoms, ground coriander and almonds with the yogurt.

2 Spoon the yogurt and spice mixture over the chicken breasts and set aside to marinate.

3 Heat the oil in a large frying pan (skillet). Add the onions to the pan and fry until a golden brown colour.

4 Add the chicken breasts to the pan, stir-frying for 5–7 minutes.

5 Add the water, cover and leave to simmer for 20–25 minutes.

6 Add the coriander (cilantro) leaves and green chillies and cook for a further 10 minutes, stirring gently from time to time.

7 Transfer to a serving plate and serve with boiled rice.

COOK'S TIP

Chicken portions may be used instead of breasts, if preferred, and should be cooked for 10 minutes longer in step 5.

Minced Lamb with Peas

Served with a dhal and rice, this simple dish makes a well-balanced meal.

6 points

NUTRITIONAL INFORMATION

Calories	304	Protein	25g
Carbohydrate	7g	Sugars	6g
Fat	26g	Saturates	6g

20 MINS 25 MINS

SERVES 4

INGREDIENTS

6 tbsp oil

1 medium onion, sliced

3 green chillies

fresh coriander (cilantro) leaves

2 tomatoes, chopped

1 tsp salt

1 tsp fresh ginger root, finely chopped

1 tsp fresh garlic, crushed

1 tsp chilli powder

450 g/1 lb lean minced lamb

100 g/3½ oz peas

1 Heat the oil in a medium-sized saucepan. Add the onion slices and fry until golden brown, stirring.

2 Add two of the green chillies, half of the fresh coriander (cilantro) leaves and the chopped tomatoes to the pan and reduce the heat to a gentle simmer.

3 Add the salt, ginger, garlic and chilli powder to the mixture in the pan and stir everything well to combine.

4 Add the minced lamb to the pan and stir-fry the mixture for 7–10 minutes, until the meat turns brown.

5 Add the peas to the mixture in the pan and cook for a further 3–4 minutes, stirring occasionally.

6 Transfer the lamb and pea mixture to warm serving plates and garnish with the remaining chopped green chilli and the fresh coriander (cilantro) leaves.

COOK'S TIP

The flavour of garlic can be changed according to how it is prepared. For instance, a whole garlic clove added to a dish will give it the flavour but not the 'bite' of chopped garlic; a halved clove will add a little bite while a finely chopped garlic clove will release most of the flavour and a crushed clove will release all of the flavour.

Spicy Lamb Chops

This is an attractive way of serving lamb chops, especially if you garnish them with potato chips, tomatoes and lemon wedges.

12.5 points

NUTRITIONAL INFORMATION

Calories 681	Protein 27g
Carbohydrate 1g	Sugars 0g
Fat 64g	Saturates 11g

15 MINS   15 MINS

SERVES 6

INGREDIENTS

1 kg/2 lb 4 oz lamb chops

2 tsp fresh ginger root, finely chopped

2 tsp fresh garlic, crushed

1 tsp pepper

1 tsp garam masala

1 tsp black cumin seeds

1½ tsp salt

850 ml/1½ pints/3¾ cups water

2 medium eggs

300 ml/½ pint/1½ cups oil

TO GARNISH

fried potato chips

tomatoes

lemon wedges

1 Using a sharp knife, trim away any excess fat from the lamb chops.

2 Mix the ginger, garlic, pepper, garam masala, cumin seeds and salt together and rub all over the chops.

3 Bring the water to a boil, add the chops and spice mixture and cook for about 45 minutes, stirring occasionally. Once the water has evaporated, remove from the heat and set aside to cool.

4 Using a fork, beat the eggs together in a large mixing bowl.

5 Heat the oil in a large saucepan.

6 Dip each lamb chop into the beaten egg and then then fry them in the saucepan for 3 minutes, turning each once.

7 Transfer the chops to a large serving dish and garnish with fried potato chips, tomatoes and lemon wedges. Serve hot.

COOK'S TIP

Garam masala is a mixture of ground spices, not an individual spice. The usual combination includes cardamom, cinnamon, cloves, cumin, nutmeg and black peppercorns, but most Indian cooks have a personal recipe, often handed down for generations. You can buy prepared garam masala at large supermarkets or Asian grocery stores.

Chicken Tossed in Black Pepper

Using black pepper instead of chilli powder produces a milder curry.
This recipe is basically a stir-fry and can be prepared in a short time.

14.5 points

NUTRITIONAL INFORMATION

Calories 736	Protein 25g	
Carbohydrate ... 16g	Sugars 4g	
Fat 64g	Saturates 15g	

15 MINS   40 MINS

SERVES 4

I N G R E D I E N T S

8 chicken thighs

1 tsp fresh ginger root, finely chopped

1 tsp fresh garlic, crushed

1 tsp salt

1½ tsp pepper

150 ml/¼ pint/⅔ cup oil

1 green (bell) pepper, roughly sliced

150 ml/¼ pint/⅔ cup water

2 tbsp lemon juice

F R I E D C O R N & P E A S

50 g/2 oz unsalted butter

200 g/8 oz frozen sweetcorn

200 g/8 oz frozen peas

½ tsp salt

½ tsp chilli powder

1 tbsp lemon juice

fresh coriander (cilantro) leaves, to garnish

1 Using a sharp knife, bone the chicken thighs, if you prefer.

2 Combine the ginger, garlic, salt and coarsely ground black pepper together in a mixing bowl.

3 Add the chicken pieces to the black pepper mixture and set aside.

4 Heat the oil in a large pan. Add the chicken and fry for 10 minutes.

5 Reduce the heat and add the green (bell) pepper and the water to the pan. Leave the mixture to simmer for 10 minutes, then sprinkle over the lemon juice.

6 Meanwhile, make the fried corn and peas. Melt the butter in a large frying pan (skillet). Add the frozen sweetcorn and peas and stir-fry, stirring occasionally, for about 10 minutes. Add the salt and chilli powder and fry for a further 5 minutes.

7 Sprinkle over the lemon juice and garnish with fresh coriander (cilantro) leaves.

8 Transfer the chicken and (bell) pepper mixture to serving plates and serve with the fried corn and peas.

Tandoori-Style Chicken

Tandoori chicken is traditionally cooked in a tandoor (clay) oven. Pre-heat the grill (broiler) to a very high temperature then lower it to medium.

9.5 points

NUTRITIONAL INFORMATION

Calories	549	Protein	43g
Carbohydrate	7g	Sugars	7g
Fat	65g	Saturates	7g

 6¼ HOURS   35 MINS

SERVES 4

INGREDIENTS

8 chicken drumsticks, skinned

150 ml/5 fl oz/⅔ cup natural yogurt

1½ tsp fresh ginger root, finely chopped

1½ tsp fresh garlic, crushed

1 tsp chilli powder

2 tsp ground cumin

2 tsp ground coriander

1 tsp salt

½ tsp red food colouring

1 tbsp tamarind paste

150 ml/¼ pint/⅔ cup water

150 ml/¼ pint/⅔ cup oil

lettuce leaves, to serve

TO GARNISH

onion rings

sliced tomatoes

lemon wedges

1 Make 2–3 slashes in each piece of chicken.

2 Place the yogurt in a bowl. Add the ginger, garlic, chilli powder, ground cumin, ground coriander, salt and red food colouring and blend until well combined.

3 Add the chicken to the yogurt and spice mixture and mix to coat well. Leave the chicken to marinate in the refrigerator for a minimum of 3 hours.

4 In a separate bowl, mix the tamarind paste with the water and fold into the yogurt and spice mixture. Toss the chicken pieces in this mixture and set aside to marinate for a further 3 hours.

5 Transfer the chicken pieces to a heatproof dish and brush the chicken with oil. Cook the chicken under a pre-heated medium-hot grill (broiler) for 30–35 minutes, turning the chicken pieces occasionally and basting with the remaining oil.

6 Arrange the chicken on a bed of lettuce and garnish with the onion rings, tomatoes and lemon wedges.

COOK'S TIP

Naan Bread (see page 55) and Mint Raita (see page 69) complement this dish perfectly.

Fried Fish in Gram Flour

Very simple to make, this fried fish dish goes very well with Tomato Curry (see page 42) and fried spicy rice.

10.5 points

NUTRITIONAL INFORMATION

Calories 637	Protein 34g
Carbohydrate 8g	Sugars 1g
Fat 52g	Saturates 5g

 15 MINS   15 MINS

SERVES 4

INGREDIENTS

100 g/3½ oz/¾ cup gram flour

1 tsp fresh ginger root, finely chopped

1 tsp fresh garlic, crushed

2 tsp chilli powder

1 tsp salt

½ tsp turmeric

2 fresh green chillies, chopped

fresh coriander (cilantro) leaves, chopped

300 ml/½ pint/1¼ cups water

1 kg/2 lb 4 oz cod

300 ml/½ pint/1¼ cups oil

cooked rice, to serve

TO GARNISH

2 lemons, cut into wedges

6 green chillies, slit down the middle

1. Place the gram flour in a large mixing bowl. Add the ginger, garlic, chilli powder, salt and turmeric and mix to blend well.

2. Add the green chillies and the coriander (cilantro) leaves to the spiced mixture and stir to mix well.

3. Pour in the water gradually and stir thoroughly to form a semi-thick batter. Set aside until it is required.

4. Using a sharp knife, cut the cod into about 8 pieces.

5. Carefully dip the pieces of cod into the batter, coating the cod all over. Gently shake off any excess batter.

6. Heat the oil in a heavy-based frying-pan (skillet). Add the battered cod and fry, in batches, over a medium heat, turning once, until cooked through and golden.

7. Transfer the battered cod to a serving dish and garnish with lemon wedges and green chillies. Serve with cooked rice.

COOK'S TIP

Gram flour or chana dhal flour (lentil flour) is used to make pakoras and to bind kebabs (kabobs). Combined with ordinary wholemeal flour it makes a delicious Indian bread.

Spicy Roast Chicken

This chicken dish, ideal for dinner parties, is cooked in the oven – which is very rare in Indian cooking. The chicken can be boned, if desired.

13 points

NUTRITIONAL INFORMATION

Calories 693   Protein 37g
Carbohydrate . . . . 8g   Sugars 6g
Fat . . . . 57g   Saturates 13g

 15 MINS   50 MINS

SERVES 4

I N G R E D I E N T S

50 g/1¾ oz/¼ cup ground almonds

50 g/1¾ oz/⅓ cup desiccated (shredded) coconut

150 ml/¼ pint/⅔ cup oil

1 medium onion, finely chopped

1 tsp fresh ginger root, chopped

1 tsp fresh garlic, crushed

1 tsp chilli powder

1½ tsp garam masala

1 tsp salt

150 ml/5 fl oz/⅔ cup yogurt

4 chicken quarters, skinned

green salad leaves, to serve

TO GARNISH

fresh coriander (cilantro) leaves

1 lemon, cut into wedges

1 In a heavy-based saucepan, dry roast the ground almonds and coconut and set aside.

2 Heat the oil in a frying pan (skillet) and fry the onion, stirring, until golden brown.

3 Place the ginger, garlic, chilli powder, garam masala and salt in a bowl and mix with the yogurt. Add the almonds and coconut and mix well.

4 Add the onions to the spice mixture, blend and set aside.

5 Arrange the chicken quarters in the bottom of a heatproof dish. Spoon the spice mixture over the chicken sparingly.

6 Cook in a pre-heated oven, 160°C/425°F/Gas Mark 3, for 35–45 minutes. Check that the chicken is cooked thoroughly by piercing the thickest part of the meat with a sharp knife or a fine skewer – the juices will run clear when the chicken is cooked through. Garnish with the coriander (cilantro) and lemon wedges and serve with a salad.

COOK'S TIP

If you want a more spicy dish, add more chilli powder and garam masala.

Prawns with Spinach

This is an attractive dish to serve as an accompaniment, especially at parties, and will also freeze well.

7 points

NUTRITIONAL INFORMATION

Calories	409	Protein	14g
Carbohydrate	2g	Sugars	2g
Fat	39g	Saturates	4g

 15 MINS   20 MINS

SERVES 4

INGREDIENTS

225 g/8 oz frozen prawns (shrimp)

350 g/12 oz canned spinach purée or frozen spinach, thawed and chopped

2 tomatoes

150 ml/¼ pint/⅔ cup oil

½ tsp mustard seeds

½ tsp onion seeds

1 tsp fresh ginger root, finely chopped

1 tsp fresh garlic, crushed

1 tsp chilli powder

1 tsp salt

1 Place the prawns (shrimp) in a bowl of cold water and set aside to defrost thoroughly.

2 Drain the can of spinach purée, if using.

3 Using a sharp knife, cut the tomatoes into slices and set aside.

4 Heat the oil in a large frying pan (skillet). Add the mustard and onion seeds to the pan.

5 Reduce the heat and add the tomatoes, spinach, ginger, garlic, chilli powder and salt to the pan and stir-fry for about 5–7 minutes.

6 Drain the prawns (shrimp) thoroughly.

7 Add the prawns (shrimp) to the spinach mixture in the pan. Gently stir the prawn (shrimp) and spinach mixture until well combined, cover and leave to simmer over a low heat for about 7–10 minutes.

8 Transfer the cooked prawns (shrimp) and spinach to a serving dish and serve hot.

COOK'S TIP

If using frozen spinach, it should be thawed and squeezed dry before using. You could use fresh spinach, if you prefer.

Lamb Pot Roast

I have always found this dish to be a great success at dinner parties, serve with rice and Potatoes with Spices & Onions (see page 44).

16 points

NUTRITIONAL INFORMATION

Calories 860	Protein 63g
Carbohydrate 4g	Sugars 2g
Fat 83g	Saturates 15g

10 MINS   3 HOURS

SERVES 6

INGREDIENTS

2.5 kg/5 lb 8 oz leg of lamb

2 tsp fresh ginger root, finely chopped

2 tsp fresh garlic, crushed

2 tsp garam masala

1 tsp salt

2 tsp black cumin seeds

4 black peppercorns

3 cloves

1 tsp chilli powder

3 tbsp lemon juice

300 ml/½ pint/1¼ cups oil

1 large onion, peeled

about 2 litres/4 pints/10 cups water

1 Remove the fat from the lamb with a sharp knife. Prick the lamb all over with a fork.

2 In a bowl, mix the ginger, garlic, garam masala, salt, black cumin seeds, peppercorns, cloves and chilli powder until well combined. Stir in the lemon juice and mix well. Then spoon the mixture over the leg of lamb and rub into the meat, making sure it is well coated, and set aside.

3 Heat the oil in a pan. Add the meat to the pan and place the onion alongside the leg of lamb.

4 Add enough water to cover the meat and cook over a low heat for 2½–3 hours, turning occasionally. (If after a while the water has evaporated and the meat is not tender, add a little extra water). Once the water has completely evaporated, turn the roast over to brown it on all sides.

5 Remove the roast from the pan and transfer to a serving dish. Cut the roast into slices or serve it whole to be carved at the table. Serve the lamb hot or cold.

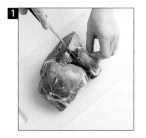

COOK'S TIP

Traditionally, a pan called a degchi is used for pot-roasting in India. It is set over hot ashes and contains hot coals in its lid.

Prawns with Tomatoes

Quick and easy to prepare, this dish is also extremely good to eat.
Use the larger tiger prawns (shrimp) for special occasions, if you prefer.

3 points

NUTRITIONAL INFORMATION

Calories	 208	Protein	.... 19g
Carbohydrate	... 13g	Sugars	.... 10g
Fat	.... 9g	Saturates	...... 1g

15 MINS   🕐 15 MINS

SERVES 4

I N G R E D I E N T S

3 medium onions

1 green (bell) pepper

1 tsp fresh ginger root, finely chopped

1 tsp fresh garlic, crushed

1 tsp salt

1 tsp chilli powder

2 tbsp lemon juice

350 g/12 oz frozen prawns (shrimp)

3 tbsp oil

400 g/14 oz can tomatoes

fresh coriander (cilantro) leaves, to garnish

1 Using a sharp knife, slice the onions and the green (bell) pepper.

2 Place the ginger, garlic, salt and chilli powder in a small bowl and mix. Add the lemon juice and mix to form a paste.

3 Place the prawns (shrimp) in a bowl of cold water and set aside to defrost. Drain thoroughly.

4 Heat the oil in a medium-sized saucepan. Add the onions and fry until golden brown.

5 Add the spice paste to the onions, reduce the heat to low and cook, stirring and mixing well, for about 3 minutes.

6 Add the tomatoes, tomato juice and the green (bell) pepper, and cook for 5–7 minutes, stirring occasionally.

7 Add the defrosted prawns (shrimp) to the pan and cook the mixture for about 10 minutes, stirring occasionally. Garnish with fresh coriander (cilantro) leaves and serve hot with plain boiled rice and a crisp green salad.

Grilled Minced Lamb

In India this is cooked on a naked flame, but I use my grill (broiler) instead and find it works just as well.

6.5 points

NUTRITIONAL INFORMATION

Calories 345   Protein 25g
Carbohydrate . . . 10g   Sugars 6g
Fat . . . . 24g   Saturates 6g

20 MINS   35 MINS

SERVES 4

INGREDIENTS

5 tbsp oil

2 onions, sliced

450 g/1 lb minced lamb

2 tbsp yogurt

1 tsp chilli powder

1 tsp fresh ginger root, finely chopped

1 tsp fresh garlic, crushed

1 tsp salt

1½ tsp garam masala

½ tsp ground allspice

2 fresh green chillies

fresh coriander (cilantro) leaves

TO GARNISH

1 onion, cut into rings

fresh coriander (cilantro) leaves, chopped

1 lemon, cut into wedges

1 Heat the oil in a saucepan. Add the sliced onions and fry until golden brown.

2 Place the minced lamb in a large bowl. Add the yogurt, chilli powder, ginger, garlic, salt, garam masala, ground allspice and mix to combine.

3 Add the lamb mixture to the fried onions and stir-fry for 10–15 minutes. Remove the mixture from the heat and set aside.

4 Meanwhile, place the green chillies and half of the coriander (cilantro) leaves in a processor and grind. Alternatively, finely chop the green chillies and coriander (cilantro) with a sharp knife. Set aside until required.

5 Put the minced lamb mixture in a food processor and grind. Alternatively, place in a large bowl and mash with a fork. Mix the lamb mixture with the chillies and coriander (cilantro) and blend well.

6 Transfer the mixture to a shallow heatproof dish. Cook under a preheated medium-hot grill (broiler) for 10–15 minutes, moving the mixture about with a fork. Watch it carefully to prevent it from burning.

7 Serve garnished with onion rings, coriander (cilantro) leaves and the lemon wedges.

Lean Lamb Cooked in Spinach

I like to serve this nutritious combination of lamb and spinach with plan boiled rice and Tomato Curry (see page 42).

16.5 points

NUTRITIONAL INFORMATION

Calories	943	Protein	31g
Carbohydrate	10g	Sugars	8g
Fat	87g	Saturates	12g

15 MINS   55 MINS

SERVES 4

INGREDIENTS

300 ml/½ pint/1¼ cups oil

2 medium onions, sliced

¼ bunch fresh coriander (cilantro)

3 green chillies, chopped

1½ tsp fresh ginger root, finely chopped

1½ tsp fresh garlic, crushed

1 tsp chilli powder

½ tsp turmeric

450 g/1 lb lean lamb, with or
without the bone

1 tsp salt

1 kg/2 lb 4 oz fresh spinach, trimmed,
washed and chopped or 425g/
15 oz can spinach

700 ml/1¼ pints/3¼ cups water

TO GARNISH

fresh red chillies, finely chopped

1 Heat the oil in a saucepan and fry the onions until they turn a pale colour.

2 Add the fresh coriander (cilantro) and 2 of the chopped green chillies to the pan and stir-fry for 3–5 minutes.

3 Reduce the heat and add the ginger, garlic, chilli powder and turmeric to the pan, stirring to mix.

4 Add the lamb to the pan and stir-fry for a further 5 minutes. Add the salt and the fresh or canned spinach and cook, stirring occasionally with a wooden spoon, for a further 3–5 minutes.

5 Add the water, stirring, and cook over a low heat, covered, for about 45 minutes. Remove the lid and check the meat. If it is not tender, turn the meat over, increase the heat and cook, uncovered, until the surplus water has been absorbed. Stir-fry the mixture for a further 5–7 minutes.

6 Transfer the lamb and spinach mixture to a serving dish and garnish with finely chopped red chillies. Serve hot.

Stuffed Tomatoes

This is an impressive dinner-party dish — serve as a starter. You will find large tomatoes are easier to fill.

6.5 points

NUTRITIONAL INFORMATION

Calories 288	Protein 16g	
Carbohydrate 5g	Sugars 5g	
Fat 23g	Saturates 9g	

 15 MINS   40 MINS

SERVES 6

INGREDIENTS

6 large, firm tomatoes

50 g/1¾ oz/4 tbsp unsalted butter

1 medium onion, finely chopped

5 tbsp oil

1 tsp fresh ginger root, finely chopped

1 tsp fresh garlic, crushed

1 tsp pepper

1 tsp salt

½ tsp garam masala

450 g/1 lb minced lamb

1 green chilli

fresh coriander (cilantro) leaves

1 Preheat the oven to 180°C/ 350°F/Gas Mark 4. Rinse the tomatoes, cut off the tops and scoop out the flesh.

2 Grease a heatproof dish with 50 g/1³/₄ oz/ 4 tbsp butter. Place the tomatoes in the dish.

3 Heat the oil in a pan and fry the onion until golden brown.

4 Lower the heat and add the ginger, garlic, pepper, salt and garam masala. Stir-fry the mixture for 3–5 minutes.

5 Add the minced lamb to the saucepan and fry for 10–15 minutes.

6 Add the green chilli and fresh coriander (cilantro) leaves and continue stir-frying the mixture for 3–5 minutes.

7 Spoon the lamb mixture into the tomatoes and replace the tops. Cook the tomatoes in the oven for 15–20 minutes.

8 Transfer the tomatoes to serving plates and serve hot.

VARIATION

You could use the same recipe to stuff red or green (bell) peppers, if you prefer.

Chicken Jalfrezi

This is a quick and tasty way to use leftover roast chicken. The sauce can also be used for any cooked poultry, lamb or beef.

5.5 points

NUTRITIONAL INFORMATION

Calories	343	Protein	42g
Carbohydrate	13g	Sugars	8g
Fat	14g	Saturates	2g

15 MINS   20 MINS

SERVES 4

INGREDIENTS

1 tsp mustard oil

3 tbsp vegetable oil

1 large onion, chopped finely

3 garlic cloves, crushed

1 tbsp tomato purée (paste)

2 tomatoes, peeled and chopped

1 tsp ground turmeric

½ tsp cumin seeds, ground

½ tsp coriander seeds, ground

½ tsp chilli powder

½ tsp garam masala

1 tsp red wine vinegar

1 small red (bell) pepper, chopped

125 g/4 oz/1 cup frozen broad (fava) beans

500 g/1 lb cooked chicken breasts, cut into bite-sized pieces

salt

fresh coriander (cilantro) sprigs, to garnish

COOK'S TIP

This dish is an ideal way of making use of leftover poultry – turkey, duck or quail. Any variety of beans works well, but vegetables are just as useful, especially root vegetables, courgettes (zucchini), potatoes or broccoli. Leafy vegetables would not be so successful.

1 Heat the mustard oil in a large frying pan (skillet) set over a high heat for about 1 minute until it begins to smoke. Add the vegetable oil, reduce the heat and then add the onion and the garlic. Fry the garlic and onion until they are golden.

2 Add the tomato purée (paste), chopped tomatoes, ground turmeric, cumin and coriander seeds, chilli powder, garam masala and red wine vinegar to the frying pan (skillet). Stir the mixture until fragrant.

3 Add the red (bell) pepper and broad (fava) beans and stir for 2 minutes until the (bell) pepper is softened. Stir in the chicken, and salt to taste. Leave the curry to simmer gently for 6–8 minutes until the chicken is heated through and the beans are tender.

4 Serve garnished with coriander (cilantro).

Chicken Tikka

For this very popular dish, small pieces of chicken are marinated for a minimum of 3 hours in yogurt and spices.

13 points

NUTRITIONAL INFORMATION

Calories 783	Protein 62g
Carbohydrate 4g	Sugars 3g
Fat 58g	Saturates 7g

 3¼ HOURS 30 MINS

SERVES 6

INGREDIENTS

1 tsp fresh ginger root, finely chopped

1 tsp fresh garlic, crushed

½ tsp ground coriander

½ tsp ground cumin

1 tsp chilli powder

3 tbsp yogurt

1 tsp salt

2 tbsp lemon juice

a few drops of red food colouring (optional)

1 tbsp tomato purée (paste)

1.5 kg/3 lb 5 oz chicken breast

1 onion, sliced

3 tbsp oil

TO GARNISH

6 lettuce leaves

1 lemon, cut into wedges

1 Blend together the ginger, garlic, ground coriander, ground cumin and chilli powder in a large mixing bowl.

2 Add the yogurt, salt, lemon juice, red food colouring (if using) and the tomato purée (paste) to the spice mixture.

3 Using a sharp knife, cut the chicken into pieces. Add the chicken to the spice mixture and toss to coat well. Leave to marinate for 3 hours, or preferably overnight.

4 Arrange the onion in the bottom of a heatproof dish. Carefully drizzle half of the oil over the onions.

5 Arrange the marinated chicken pieces on top of the onions and cook them under a pre-heated grill (broiler), turning each piece once and basting with the remaining oil, for 25–30 minutes.

6 Serve the chicken tikka on a bed of lettuce and garnish with the lemon wedges.

COOK'S TIP

Chicken Tikka can be served with Naan Breads (see page 55), Raita (see page 69) and Mango Chutney (see page 65) or as a starter.

Spicy Lamb Curry in Sauce

This curry is especially good served with plain boiled rice and Onion Dhal (see page 48).

NUTRITIONAL INFORMATION

Calories 1251   Protein 43g

Carbohydrate .... 9g   Sugars 7g

Fat .... 143g   Saturates 18g

🍚 25 MINS   🕐 1 HOUR

SERVES 4

INGREDIENTS

2 tsp ground cumin

2 tsp ground coriander

2 tsp desiccated (shredded) coconut

1 tsp mixed mustard and onion seeds

2 tsp sesame seeds

1 tsp fresh ginger root, finely chopped

1 tsp fresh garlic, crushed

1 tsp chilli powder

1 tsp salt

450 g/1 lb lean lamb, cubed

450 ml/16 fl oz/2 cups oil

3 medium onions, sliced

850 ml/1½ pints/3¾ cups water

2 tbsp lemon juice

4 green chillies, split

1 Dry roast the ground cumin, ground coriander, desiccated (shredded) coconut, mixed mustard and onion seeds and the sesame seeds in a heavy frying pan (skillet), shaking the pan frequently to stop the spices from burning. Then grind the roasted spices using a pestle and mortar.

2 In a large mixing bowl, blend together the roasted ground spices along with the ginger, garlic, chilli powder, salt and the cubed lamb and set aside.

3 In a separate pan, heat 300 ml/½ pint/1½ cups of oil and fry the onions until golden brown.

4 Add the meat mixture to the onions and stir-fry for 5–7 minutes over a low heat. Add the water and simmer for 45 minutes, stirring occasionally. When the meat is cooked through, remove from the heat and sprinkle with lemon juice.

5 In a separate saucepan, heat the remaining oil and add the four split green chillies. Reduce the heat and cover with a lid. Remove the pan from the heat after about 30 seconds and set aside to cool.

6 Pour the chilli oil mixture over the meat curry and serve hot with Onion Dhal (see page 48) and plain boiled rice.

Pork & Mushroom Curry

Vary the meat used here according to personal taste, using lean leg or shoulder of lamb or braising beef instead of pork.

NUTRITIONAL INFORMATION

Calories 560	Protein 46g	
Carbohydrate . . . 14g	Sugars 11g	
Fat 36g	Saturates 13g	

25 MINS   1¾ HOURS

SERVES 4

INGREDIENTS

750 g/1 lb 10 oz leg or shoulder of pork

3 tbsp vegetable oil

2 onions, sliced

2 garlic cloves, crushed

2.5 cm/1 inch piece ginger root, chopped finely

2 fresh green chillies, seeded and chopped, or use 1–2 tsp minced chilli (from a jar)

1½ tbsp medium curry paste

1 tsp ground coriander

175–250 g/6–9 oz mushrooms, sliced thickly

850 ml/1½ pints/3½ cups stock

3 tomatoes, chopped

½–1 tsp salt

60 g/2 oz creamed coconut, chopped

2 tbsp ground almonds

TO GARNISH

2 tbsp vegetable oil

1 green or red (bell) pepper, seeded and cut into thin strips

6 spring onions (scallions), trimmed and sliced

1 tsp cumin seeds

1 Cut the pork into small bite-sized pieces. Heat the oil in a saucepan and fry the pork until sealed, stirring frequently. Remove the pork from the pan.

2 Add the onions, garlic, ginger, chillies, curry paste and ground coriander to the saucepan and cook gently for 2 minutes. Stir in the mushrooms, stock and tomatoes, and season with a little salt according to taste.

3 Return the pork to the pan, then cover and simmer very gently for 1¼–1½ hours or until the pork is tender.

4 Stir the creamed coconut and ground almonds into the curry, then cover the pan and cook gently for 3 minutes.

5 Meanwhile, make the garnish. Heat the oil in a frying pan (skillet), add the (bell) pepper strips and spring onion (scallion) slices and fry gently until glistening and tender-crisp. Stir in the cumin seeds and fry for 30 seconds. Spoon over the curry and serve.

Beef Cooked in Whole Spices

This is a delicious way of cooking beef. The fragrant whole spices perfectly complement the meat.

NUTRITIONAL INFORMATION

Calories . . . . 900 Protein 30g
Carbohydrate . . . 13g Sugars 10g
Fat . . . . 81g Saturates 10g

 15 MINS   1½ HOURS

SERVES 4

I N G R E D I E N T S

300 ml/½ pint/1¼ cups oil

3 medium onions, chopped finely

2.5 cm/1 inch ginger root, shredded

4 cloves garlic, shredded

2 cinnamon sticks

3 whole green cardamoms

3 whole cloves

4 whole black peppercorns

6 dried red chillies, chopped

150 ml/5 fl oz/⅔ cup yogurt

450 g/1 lb beef, with or without bone, cut into cubes

3 green chillies, chopped

600 ml/1 pint/2½ cups water

fresh coriander (cilantro) leaves

1 Heat the oil in a frying pan (skillet) and fry the onions, stirring, until golden brown.

2 Reduce the heat and add the ginger, garlic, cinnamon sticks, green cardamoms, cloves, black peppercorns and red chillies to the pan and stir-fry for 5 minutes.

3 In a bowl, whip the yogurt with a fork. Add the yogurt to the onions and stir to combine.

4 Add the meat and 2 of the green chillies to the frying pan (skillet) and stir-fry the mixture for 5–7 minutes.

5 Gradually add the water to the pan, stirring well. Cover the pan and cook the beef and spice mixture for 1 hour, stirring and adding more water if necessary.

6 When thoroughly cooked through, remove the pan from the heat and transfer the beef and spice mixture to a serving dish. Garnish with the remaining chopped green chilli and the fresh coriander (cilantro) leaves.

VARIATION

Substitute lamb for the beef in this recipe, if you prefer.

Tomatoes with Meat & Yogurt

One of my favourites, this delicious tomato korma has a semi-thick sauce. I like to serve freshly made chapatis with it.

NUTRITIONAL INFORMATION

Calories 1184	Protein 57g
Carbohydrate ... 22g	Sugars 17g
Fat 97g	Saturates 18g

15 MINS   1 HR 25 MINS

SERVES 2

INGREDIENTS

1 tsp garam masala

1 tsp fresh ginger root, finely chopped

1 tsp fresh garlic, crushed

2 black cardamoms

1 tsp chilli powder

½ tsp black cumin seeds

2 x 2.5 cm/1–inch cinnamon sticks

1 tsp salt

150 ml/5 fl oz/⅔ cup natural yogurt

½ kg/1 lb 2 oz lean cubed lamb

150 ml/¼ pint/⅔ cup oil

2 onions, sliced

600 ml/1 pint/2½ cups water

2 firm tomatoes, cut into quarters

2 tbsp lemon juice

TO GARNISH

fresh coriander (cilantro) leaves, chopped

2 green chillies, chopped

COOK'S TIP

Kormas are slowly braised dishes, many of which are the rich and spicy, Persian-inspired Mogul dishes served on special occasions. In a properly cooked korma, prime, tender cuts of meat are used, and the small amout of cooking liquid is absorbed back into the meat to produce a succulent result.

1 In a large bowl, mix together the garam masala, ginger, garlic, cardamoms, chilli powder, black cumin seeds, cinnamon sticks, salt and yogurt until well combined.

2 Add the meat to the bowl and mix well to coat the meat. Set aside.

3 Heat the oil in a large saucepan and fry the onions until golden brown.

4 Add the meat to the pan and stir-fry for about 5 minutes. Reduce the heat, add the water, cover and simmer for about 1 hour, stirring occasionally.

5 Add the tomatoes and sprinkle with lemon juice. Leave to simmer for a further 7–10 minutes.

6 Garnish with coriander (cilantro) leaves and green chillies. Serve hot.

Lamb Curry in a Thick Sauce

Originally a Kashmiri dish, this lamb stew is now made all over India. It is noted for its delicious tomato-flavoured sauce and is ideal for a dinner party.

14 points

NUTRITIONAL INFORMATION

Calories 797	Protein 33g	
Carbohydrate . . . 12g	Sugars 9g	
Fat 69g	Saturates 11g	

15 MINS   55 MINS

SERVES 6

I N G R E D I E N T S

1 kg/2 lb 4 oz lean lamb, with or without bone

7 tbsp yogurt

75 g/2¾ oz/5 tbsp almonds

2 tsp garam masala

2 tsp fresh ginger root, finely chopped

2 tsp fresh garlic, crushed

1½ tsp chilli powder

1½ tsp salt

300 ml/½ pint/1¼ cups oil

3 onions, finely chopped

4 green cardamoms

2 bay leaves

3 green chillies, chopped

2 tbsp lemon juice

400 g/14 oz can tomatoes

300 ml/½ pint/1¼ cups water

fresh coriander (cilantro) leaves, chopped

1 Using a sharp knife, cut the lamb into small, even-sized pieces.

2 In a large mixing bowl, combine the yogurt, almonds, garam masala, ginger, garlic, chilli powder and salt, stirring to mix the ingredients well.

3 Heat the oil in a large saucepan and fry the onions with the cardamoms and the bay leaves until golden brown, stirring constantly.

4 Add the meat and the yogurt mixture to the pan and stir-fry for 3–5 minutes.

5 Add 2 of the chopped green chillies, the lemon juice and the canned tomatoes to the mixture in the pan and stir-fry for a further 5 minutes.

6 Add the water to the pan. Then cover the curry and leave to simmer gently over a low heat for 35–40 minutes.

7 Add the remaining green chilli and the coriander (cilantro) leaves and stir until the sauce has thickened. (Remove the lid and turn the heat higher if the sauce is too watery).

8 Transfer the curry to warm serving plates and serve hot.

Cubed Lamb Kebabs

In India these kebabs (kabobs) are traditionally served in the evening as you sit out in the open – they are barbecued (grilled) as you watch, to order.

5 points

NUTRITIONAL INFORMATION

Calories	258	Protein	27g
Carbohydrate	7g	Sugars	6g
Fat	14g	Saturates	5g

 3¼ HRS   30 MINS

SERVES 8

INGREDIENTS

1 kg/2 lb 4 oz lean lamb, boned and cubed

1 tsp meat tenderizer

1½ tsp fresh ginger root, finely chopped

1½ tsp fresh garlic, crushed

1 tsp chilli powder

½ tsp turmeric

½ tsp salt

2 tbsp water

8 tomatoes, cut in half

8 small pickling onions

16 mushrooms

1 green (bell) pepper, cut into large pieces

1 red (bell) pepper, cut into large pieces

2 tbsp oil

2 lemons, cut into quarters, to garnish

1 Wash the cubed lamb and place it in a clean dish. Apply the tenderizer to the meat, using your hands. Then set the dish aside for about 3 hours at room temperature.

2 Mix together the ginger, garlic, chilli powder, turmeric and salt in a bowl. Add the water and mix with the spices to form a paste. Add the cubed meat and mix until it is well coated with the spice mixture.

3 Arrange the meat cubes on skewers, alternating with the tomatoes, pickling onions, mushrooms and (bell) peppers. Brush the meat and vegetables with the oil.

4 Grill (broil) the kebabs (kabobs) under a pre-heated grill (broiler) for 25–30 minutes or until the meat is cooked through. When cooked, remove the kebabs (kabobs) from the grill (broiler) and transfer to a serving plate. Arrange lemon wedges on the side and serve immediately with boiled rice and a Raita (see page 69).

COOK'S TIP

If using wooden skewers, soak them in cold water for 20 minutes before they are used to prevent them from burning during cooking.

Chicken & Onions

This dish represents one of the rare occasions when we do not use yogurt to cook chicken. It is perfect served with Pulao Rice (see page 53).

9.5 points

NUTRITIONAL INFORMATION

Calories 553	Protein 24g
Carbohydrate . . . 15g	Sugars 11g
Fat 45g	Saturates 6g

 15 MINS   35 MINS

SERVES 4

I N G R E D I E N T S

300 ml/½ pint/1¼ cups oil

4 medium onions, finely chopped

1½ tsp fresh ginger root, finely chopped

1½ tsp garam masala

1½ tsp fresh garlic, crushed

1 tsp chilli powder

1 tsp ground coriander

3 whole cardamoms

3 peppercorns

3 tbsp tomato purée (paste)

8 chicken thighs, skinned

300 ml/½ pint/1¼ cups water

2 tbsp lemon juice

1 green chilli

fresh coriander (cilantro) leaves

green chilli strips, to garnish

1 Heat the oil in a large frying pan (skillet). Add the onion and fry, stirring occasionally, until golden brown.

2 Reduce the heat and add the ginger, garam masala, garlic, chilli powder, ground coriander, whole cardamoms and the peppercorns, stirring well to mix.

3 Add the tomato purée (paste) to the mixture in the frying pan (skillet) and stir-fry with the spices for 5–7 minutes.

4 Add the chicken thighs to the pan and toss in the spice mixture to coat them thoroughly.

5 Pour the water into the saucepan, cover and leave the curry to simmer for 20–25 minutes.

6 Add the lemon juice, green chilli and coriander (cilantro) to the mixture, and combine.

7 Transfer the chicken and onions to warmed serving plates, garnish and serve hot.

COOK'S TIP

A dish of meat cooked with plenty of onions is called a Do Pyaza. This curry definitely improves if made in advance and then reheated before serving. This develops a deeper flavour.

Buttered Chicken

A simple and mouth-watering dish with a lovely thick sauce, this makes an impressive centrepiece for a dinner party.

13.5 points

NUTRITIONAL INFORMATION

Calories	612	Protein	65g
Carbohydrate	13g	Sugars	10g
Fat	34g	Saturates	19g

 15 MINS   1 HR 5 MINS

SERVES 4

INGREDIENTS

100 g/3½ oz/8 tbsp unsalted butter

1 tbsp oil

2 medium onions, finely chopped

1 tsp fresh ginger root, finely chopped

2 tsp garam masala

2 tsp ground coriander

1 tsp chilli powder

1 tsp black cumin seeds

1 tsp fresh garlic, crushed

1 tsp salt

3 whole green cardamoms

3 whole black peppercorns

150 ml/5 fl oz/⅔ cup natural yogurt

2 tbsp tomato purée (paste)

8 chicken pieces, skinned

150 ml/¼ pint/⅔ cup water

2 whole bay leaves

150 ml/5 fl oz/⅔ cup single (light) cream

TO GARNISH

fresh coriander (cilantro) leaves

2 green chillies, chopped

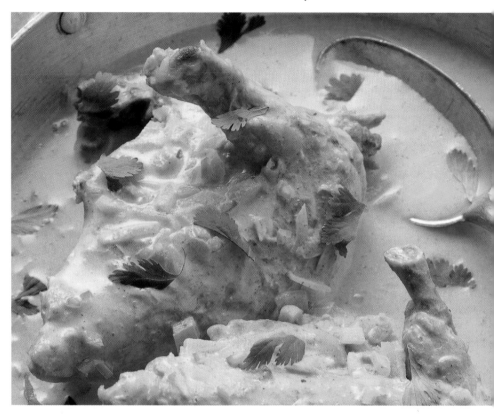

1 Heat the butter and oil in a large frying pan (skillet). Add the onions and fry until golden, stirring. Reduce the heat.

2 Crush the fresh ginger and place in a bowl. Add the garam masala, ground coriander, ginger, chilli powder, black cumin seeds, garlic, salt, cardamoms and black peppercorns and blend. Add the yogurt and tomato purée (paste) and stir to combine.

3 Add the chicken pieces to the yogurt and spice mixture and stir them to coat well.

4 Add the chicken to the onions in the pan and stir-fry vigorously, making semi-circular movements, for 5–7 minutes.

5 Add the water and the bay leaves to the mixture in the pan and leave to simmer for 30 minutes, stirring occasionally.

6 Add the cream and cook for a further 10–15 minutes.

7 Garnish with fresh coriander (cilantro) and chillies and serve hot.

Bengali-Style Fish

Fresh fish is eaten a great deal in Bengal (Bangladesh), and this dish is made with mustard oil which gives the fish a good flavour.

9 points

NUTRITIONAL INFORMATION

Calories	534	Protein	47g
Carbohydrate	8g	Sugars	6g
Fat	35g	Saturates	5g

20 MINS · 40 MINS

SERVES 4

I N G R E D I E N T S

1 tsp turmeric

1 tsp salt

1 kg/2 lb 4 oz cod fillet, skinned and cut into pieces

6 tbsp corn oil

4 green chillies

1 tsp fresh ginger root, finely chopped

1 tsp fresh garlic, crushed

2 medium onions, finely chopped

2 tomatoes, finely chopped

6 tbsp mustard oil

450 ml/¾ pint/2 cups water

fresh coriander (cilantro) leaves, chopped, to garnish

1 Mix together the turmeric and salt in a small bowl.

2 Spoon the turmeric and salt mixture over the fish pieces.

3 Heat the oil in a frying-pan (skillet) and fry the fish pieces until pale yellow. Remove the fish with a perforated spoon and set aside.

4 Place the green chillies, ginger, garlic, onions, tomatoes and mustard oil in a pestle and mortar and grind to form a paste. Alternatively, work the ingredients in a food processor.

5 Transfer the spice paste to a saucepan and dry-fry until golden brown.

6 Remove the pan from the heat and gently place the fish pieces into the paste without breaking the fish up.

7 Return the pan to the heat, add the water and cook the fish, uncovered, over a medium heat for 15–20 minutes.

8 Garnish with chopped coriander (cilantro).

COOK'S TIP

In the hot and humid eastern plains that surround Bengal, the mustard plant flourishes, providing oil for cooking and spicy seeds for flavouring. Fish and seafood appear in many meals, often flavoured with mustard oil.

Sheekh Kebabs

These minced lamb kebabs (kabobs) should ideally be barbecued (grilled), on skewers, but grilling (broiling) works just as well.

1.5 points

NUTRITIONAL INFORMATION

Calories	82	Protein	10g
Carbohydrate	2g	Sugars	1g
Fat	4g	Saturates	2g

  3¼ HRS   15 MINS

SERVES 10

INGREDIENTS

2 tsp meat tenderizer

450 g/1 lb lean minced lamb

fresh coriander (cilantro) leaves

1 medium onion, finely chopped

2 green chillies, finely chopped

2 tbsp yogurt

1 tsp fresh ginger root, finely chopped

1 tsp fresh garlic, crushed

1 tsp ground cumin

1 tsp ground coriander

½ tsp salt

1 tsp chilli powder

½ tsp ground allspice

1 tsp garam masala

chilli powder, to garnish

lemon wedges

VATIATION

These kababs (kabobs) are delicious cooked over a barbecue (grill). Serve in pitta bread for a party dish or add the meat to a salad.

1 Apply the meat tenderizer to the minced lamb with your fingers and blend in well. Set aside for at least 3 hours.

2 Meanwhile, chop the coriander (cilantro) finely. Mix the onion, green chillies and coriander (cilantro) in a bowl.

3 In a separate bowl, mix the yogurt with the ginger, garlic, ground cumin, ground coriander, salt, chilli powder, ground allspice and garam masala. Then blend this with the onion mixture.

4 Blend the combined mixture into the minced lamb and mix together with your hands. Divide the mixture into 10–12 equal portions. Roll each portion around a skewer with your fingers, gently pressing all around.

5 Grill (broil) the lamb kebabs (kabobs) under a pre-heated medium grill (broiler), basting with the oil occasionally.

6 Sprinkle with chilli powder and serve with lemon wedges and a Raita (see page 69).

Meatballs in Sauce

This is an old family recipe. The koftas (meatballs) are easy to make and also freeze beautifully.

11.5 points

NUTRITIONAL INFORMATION

Calories	644	Protein	.......27g
Carbohydrate	...16g	Sugars	.......10g
Fat	..........54g	Saturates	......9g

 15 MINS   30 MINS

SERVES 4

I N G R E D I E N T S

450 g/1 lb minced lamb

1 tsp fresh ginger root, crushed

1 tsp fresh garlic, crushed

1 tsp garam masala

1½ tsp poppy seeds

1 tsp salt

½ tsp chilli powder

1 medium onion, finely chopped

1 green chilli, finely chopped

fresh coriander (cilantro) leaves

1 tbsp gram flour

150 ml/¼ pint/⅔ cup oil

S A U C E

2 tbsp oil

3 medium onions, finely chopped

2 small cinnamon sticks

2 large black cardamoms

1 tsp fresh ginger root, finely chopped

1 tsp fresh garlic, crushed

1 tsp salt

75 ml/3 fl oz/4½ tbsp natural yogurt

150 ml/¼ pint/⅔ cup water

T O   G A R N I S H

fresh coriander (cilantro) leaves, finely chopped

1 green chilli, finely chopped

1 Place the lamb in a large mixing bowl. Add the ginger, garlic, garam masala, poppy seeds, salt, chilli powder, onion, chilli, coriander (cilantro) and gram flour and mix well with a fork.

2 Make small meatballs out of the mixture with your hands; set aside.

3 To make the sauce, heat the oil and fry the onions until golden brown. Add the cinnamon sticks and cardamoms to the pan, lower the heat and stir-fry for a further 5 minutes. Add the ginger, garlic, salt, yogurt and water; mix well.

4 Transfer to a serving bowl and garnish with chopped coriander (cilantro) and chillies.

5 Heat the oil and fry the meatballs for 8–10 minutes or until golden brown.

6 Transfer the meatballs to warm plates. Serve with the sauce and Indian bread.

Prawns with Peppers

This is a colourful and impressive side dish. As there are not many spices in this recipe I like to use a lot of fresh coriander (cilantro) in it.

6 points

NUTRITIONAL INFORMATION

Calories 247   Protein 22g
Carbohydrate . . . . 4g   Sugars 3g
Fat . . . . 16g   Saturates 10g

 15 MINS   20 MINS

SERVES 4

I N G R E D I E N T S

450 g/1 lb frozen prawns (shrimp)

½ bunch fresh coriander (cilantro) leaves

1 tsp fresh garlic, crushed

1 tsp salt

1 medium green (bell) pepper, sliced

1 medium red (bell) pepper

75 g/2¾ oz/5½ tbsp unsalted butter

1 Defrost the prawns (shrimp). Once they are completely thawed, rinse them under cold running water twice. Drain the prawns (shrimp) thoroughly and place in a large mixing bowl.

2 Using a sharp knife, finely chop the bunch of fresh coriander (cilantro) leaves.

3 Add the garlic, salt and fresh, chopped coriander (cilantro) leaves to the prawns (shrimp), then set the bowl aside until required.

4 Deseed the (bell) peppers and cut into thin slices, using a sharp knife.

5 Melt the butter in a large frying pan (skillet). Add the prawns (shrimp) to the pan and stir-fry, stirring and tossing the prawns (shrimp) gently, for 10–12 minutes.

6 Add the (bell) peppers to the pan and fry for a further 3–5 minutes, stirring occasionally.

7 Transfer the prawns (shrimp) and (bell) peppers to a serving dish and serve hot.

VARIATION

You could use large tiger prawns (shrimp) in this dish, if you prefer.

Meat-Coated Eggs

These are ideal for taking on a picnic, because they are dry. In fact, they are the Indian equivalent of the Scotch egg.

5.5 pants

NUTRITIONAL INFORMATION

Calories .... 288 Protein 25g
Carbohydrate .... 3g Sugars 1g
Fat .... 20g Saturates 6g

55 MINS   15 MINS

SERVES 6

INGREDIENTS

450 g/1 lb lean minced lamb

1 small onion, finely chopped

1 green chilli, finely chopped

1 tsp fresh ginger root, finely chopped

1 tsp fresh garlic, crushed

1 tsp ground coriander

1 tsp garam masala

1 tsp salt

1½ tbsp gram flour

7 eggs, 6 of them hard–boiled
   (hard–cooked) and shelled, 1 beaten

oil, for deep-frying

1 Place the lamb, onion and the green chilli in a bowl and mix together. Transfer the mixture to a food processor and work until well ground. (Alternatively, grind the mixture by hand using a pestle and mortar).

2 Remove the mixture from the food processor and add the ginger, garlic, ground coriander, garam masala, salt, gram flour and the beaten egg. Combine all the ingredients together with your hands.

3 Divide the mixture into 6 equal portions. Roll each portion out to form a flat round, about 5 mm/¼ inch thick. Place a hard–boiled (hard–cooked) egg in the middle of each round and wrap the meat mixture around the egg to enclose it completely. When all 6 eggs have been covered, set aside in a cool place for 20–30 minutes.

4 Meanwhile, heat the oil in a karahi or deep frying pan (skillet). Gently drop the meat-coated eggs into the oil and fry for 2–4 minutes or until golden brown. Using a perforated spoon, remove the meat-coated eggs from the oil, transfer to kitchen paper and drain thoroughly. Serve hot.

VARIATION

If you wish to serve these Meat-Coated Eggs in a sauce, use the recipe for Meatballs in Sauce (see page 31).

Beef Korma with Almonds

This korma, a traditional northern Indian recipe, has a thick sauce and is quite simple to cook.

16.5 points

NUTRITIONAL INFORMATION

Calories 988	Protein 51g
Carbohydrate ... 39g	Sugars 6g
Fat 70g	Saturates 9g

20 MINS   1½ HOURS

SERVES 6

I N G R E D I E N T S

300 ml/½ pint/1¼ cups oil

3 medium onions, finely chopped

1 kg/2 lb 4 oz lean beef, cubed

1½ tsp garam masala

1½ tsp ground coriander

1½ tsp fresh ginger root, finely chopped

1½ tsp fresh garlic, crushed

1 tsp salt

150 ml/5 fl oz/⅔ cup natural yogurt

2 cloves

3 green cardamoms

4 black peppercorns

600 ml/1 pint/2½ cups water

TO GARNISH

6 almonds, soaked, peeled and chopped

2 green chillies, chopped

a few fresh coriander (cilantro) leaves

1 Heat the oil in a saucepan. Add the onions and stir-fry until golden brown. Remove half of the onions from the pan, set aside and reserve.

2 Add the meat to the remaining onions in the pan and stir-fry for about 5 minutes. Remove the pan from the heat.

3 Mix the garam masala, ground coriander, ginger, garlic, salt and yogurt in a bowl. Gradually add the meat to the yogurt and spice mixture and mix to coat the meat on all sides. Place in the saucepan, return to the heat, and stir-fry for 5–7 minutes, or until the mixture is nearly brown in colour.

4 Add the cloves, green cardamoms and black peppercorns. Add the water, lower the heat, cover and leave to simmer for about 45–60 minutes. If the water has completely evaporated but the meat is still not tender enough, add another 300 ml/½ pint/1½ cups water and cook for a further 10–15 minutes, stirring occasionally.

5 Just before serving, garnish with the reserved onions, chopped almonds, green chillies and the fresh coriander (cilantro) leaves. Serve with Indian bread.

Okra Curry

This is a delicious dry bhujia (vegetarian curry). As okra is such a tasty vegetable it does not need many spices.

7 points

NUTRITIONAL INFORMATION

Calories 405	Protein 4g
Carbohydrate ... 10g	Sugars 8g
Fat 39g	Saturates 4g

15 MINS   30 MINS

SERVES 4

I N G R E D I E N T S

450 g/1 lb okra (lady's fingers)

150 ml/¼ pint/⅔ cup oil

2 medium onions, sliced

3 green chillies, finely chopped

2 curry leaves

1 tsp salt

1 tomato, sliced

2 tbsp lemon juice

fresh coriander (cilantro) leaves

  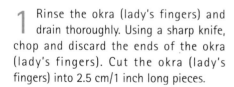

1 Rinse the okra (lady's fingers) and drain thoroughly. Using a sharp knife, chop and discard the ends of the okra (lady's fingers). Cut the okra (lady's fingers) into 2.5 cm/1 inch long pieces.

2 Heat the oil in a large, heavy frying-pan (skillet). Add the onions, green chillies, curry leaves and salt and mix together. Stir-fry the vegetables for 5 minutes.

3 Gradually add the okra (lady's fingers), mixing in gently with a perforated spoon. Stir-fry the vegetable mixture over a medium heat for 12–15 minutes.

4 Add the sliced tomato to the mixture and sprinkle over the lemon juice sparingly.

5 Garnish with coriander (cilantro) leaves, cover and leave to simmer for 3–5 minutes.

6 Transfer to serving plates and serve hot.

COOK'S TIP

When you buy fresh okra (lady's fingers), make sure they are not shriveled and that they do not have any brown spots. Fresh okra (lady's fingers) will keep, tightly wrapped, for up to 3 days in the refrigerator. Okra (lady's fingers) have a remarkable glutinous quality which naturally thickens curries and casseroles.

Potato Curry

Served hot with Pooris (see page 51), this curry makes an excellent brunch with Mango Chutney (see page 65) as an accompaniment.

7.5 points

NUTRITIONAL INFORMATION

Calories 441	Protein 35g	
Carbohydrate ... 24g	Sugars 2g	
Fat 38g	Saturates 4g	

15 MINS   20 MINS

SERVES 4

INGREDIENTS

3 medium potatoes

150 ml/¼ pint/⅔ cup oil

1 tsp onion seeds

½ tsp fennel seeds

4 curry leaves

1 tsp ground cumin

1 tsp ground coriander

1 tsp chilli powder

1 pinch turmeric

1 tsp salt

1½ tsp aamchoor (dried mango powder)

1 Peel and rinse the potatoes. Using a sharp knife, cut each potato into six slices.

2 Boil the potato slices in a saucepan of water for about 12–15 minutes, until they are just cooked, but not mushy (test by piercing with a sharp knife or a skewer). Drain and set aside until required.

COOK'S TIP

Traditionally, semolina dessert is served to follow Potato Curry.

3 In a separate saucepan heat the oil. Reduce the heat and add the onion seeds, the fennel seeds and the curry leaves, stirring them continuously

4 Remove the pan from the heat and add the ground cumin, coriander, chilli powder, turmeric, salt and the aamchoor (dried mango powder), stirring well to combine.

5 Return the pan to the heat and stir-fry the spicy mixture for about 1 minute.

6 Pour this mixture over the cooked potatoes, mix together well without breaking up the potatoes too much, and stir-fry over a low heat for about 5 minutes.

7 Transfer the potato curry to serving dishes and serve immediately.

Green Pumpkin Curry

The Indian pumpkin used in this curry is long and green and sold by weight. It can easily be bought from any Indian or Pakistani grocers.

6.5 points

NUTRITIONAL INFORMATION

Calories 386   Protein 2g
Carbohydrate . . . 10g   Sugars 8g
Fat . . . . 38g   Saturates 4g

🍢 15 MINS   🕐 25 MINS

SERVES 4

I N G R E D I E N T S

150 ml/¼ pint/⅔ cup oil

2 medium-sized onions, sliced

½ tsp white cumin seeds

450 g/1 lb green pumpkin, cubed

1 tsp aamchoor (dried mango powder)

1 tsp fresh ginger root, finely chopped

1 tsp fresh garlic, crushed

1 tsp crushed red chilli

½ tsp salt

300 ml/½ pint/1¼ cups water

1 Heat the oil in a large frying pan (skillet). Add the onions and cumin seeds and fry, stirring occasionally, until a light golden brown colour.

2 Add the cubed pumpkin to the pan and stir-fry for 3–5 minutes over a low heat.

3 Mix the aamchoor (dried mango powder), ginger, garlic, chilli and salt.

4 Add the spice mixture to the onion mixture, stirring well to combine.

5 Add the water, cover and cook over a low heat for 10–15 minutes, stirring occasionally.

6 Transfer to serving plates and serve with Gram Flour Bread (see page 58).

COOK'S TIP

Cumin seeds are popular with Indian cooks because of their warm, pungent flavour and aroma. The seeds are sold whole or ground, and are usually included as one of the flavourings in garam masala. You can use ordinary pumpkin for this recipe, if you prefer.

Mixed Vegetables

This is one of my favourite vegetarian recipes. You can make it with any vegetables you choose, but I think the combination below is ideal.

1.3.5 points

NUTRITIONAL INFORMATION

Calories 812	Protein 6g	
Carbohydrate . . . 28g	Sugars 11g	
Fat 77g	Saturates 8g	

🍲 15 MINS   🕐 50 MINS

SERVES 4

INGREDIENTS

300 ml/½ pint/1¼ cups oil

1 tsp mustard seeds

1 tsp onion seeds

½ tsp white cumin seeds

3–4 curry leaves, chopped

450 g/1 lb onions, finely chopped

3 medium tomatoes, chopped

½ red, ½ green (bell) pepper, sliced

1 tsp fresh ginger root, finely chopped

1 tsp fresh garlic, crushed

1 tsp chilli powder

¼ tsp turmeric

1 tsp salt

425 ml/¾ pint/2 cups water

2 medium potatoes, peeled and cut into pieces

½ cauliflower, cut into small florets

4 medium carrots, peeled and sliced

3 green chillies, finely chopped

fresh coriander (cilantro) leaves

1 tbsp lemon juice

1 Heat the oil in a large saucepan. Add the mustard, onion and white cumin seeds along with the curry leaves and fry until they turn a shade darker.

2 Add the onions to the pan and fry over a medium heat until golden.

3 Add the tomatoes and (bell) peppers and stir-fry for about 5 minutes.

4 Add the ginger, garlic, chilli powder, turmeric and salt and mix well.

5 Add 300 ml/½ pint/1¼ cups of the water, cover and leave to simmer for 10–12 minutes.

6 Add the potatoes, cauliflower, carrots, green chillies and coriander (cilantro) leaves and stir-fry for about 5 minutes.

7 Add the remaining 150 ml/¼ pint/⅔ cup of water and the lemon juice, stirring to combine. Cover and leave to simmer for about 15 minutes, stirring occasionally.

8 Transfer the mixed vegetables to serving plates and serve at once.

Fried Cauliflower

A dry dish flavoured with a few herbs, this is a very versatile accompaniment.

2 points

NUTRITIONAL INFORMATION

Calories	137	Protein	4g
Carbohydrate	4g	Sugars	4g
Fat	12g	Saturates	1g

10 MINS   20 MINS

SERVES 4

INGREDIENTS

4 tbsp oil

½ tsp onion seeds

½ tsp mustard seeds

½ tsp fenugreek seeds

4 dried red chillies

1 small cauliflower, cut into small florets

1 tsp salt

1 green (bell) pepper, diced

1 Heat the oil in a large, heavy-based saucepan.

2 Add the onion seeds, mustard seeds, fenugreek seeds and the dried red chillies to the pan, stirring to mix.

3 Reduce the heat and gradually add all of the cauliflower and the salt to the pan. Stir-fry the mixture for 7–10 minutes, coating the cauliflower florets thoroughly in the spice mixture.

4 Add the diced green (bell) pepper to the pan and stir-fry the mixture for 3–5 minutes.

5 Transfer the spicy fried cauliflower to a serving dish and serve hot.

VATIATION

For a weekend feast or a special occasion, this dish looks great made with baby cauliflowers instead of florets. Baby vegetables are more widely available nowadays, and the baby cauliflowers look very appealing on the plate. Peel off most of the outer leaves, leaving a few small leaves for decoration. Blanch the baby cauliflowers whole for 4 minutes and continue from step 3.

Courgettes & Fenugreek Seeds

This delicious curry contains fenugreek seeds which have a beautiful aroma and a distinctive taste.

3.5 points

NUTRITIONAL INFORMATION

Calories 193	Protein 4g
Carbohydrate 7g	Sugars 5g
Fat 17g	Saturates 2g

 15 MINS   15 MINS

SERVES 4

INGREDIENTS

6 tbsp oil

1 medium onion, finely chopped

3 green chillies, finely chopped

1 tsp fresh ginger root, finely chopped

1 tsp fresh garlic, crushed

1 tsp chilli powder

450 g/1 lb courgettes (zucchini), sliced

2 tomatoes, sliced

fresh coriander (cilantro) leaves, plus extra to garnish

2 tsp fenugreek seeds

1 Heat the oil in a large frying pan (skillet).

2 Add the onion, green chillies, ginger, garlic and chilli powder to the pan, stirring well to combine.

3 Add the sliced courgettes (zucchini) and the sliced tomatoes to the pan and stir-fry for 5–7 minutes.

4 Add the cilantro (coriander) and fenugreek seeds to the courgette (zucchini) mixture in the pan and stir-fry for 5 minutes.

5 Remove the pan from the heat and transfer the courgette (zucchini) and fenugreek seed mixture to serving dishes. Garnish and serve hot with chapatis.

COOK'S TIP

Both the leaves and seeds of fenugreek are used, but the stalks and root should be discarded, as they have a bitter taste. Fresh fenugreek is sold in bunches. Fenugreek seeds are flat and yellowish brown in colour. You could use coriander seeds instead of the fenugreek seeds, if you prefer.

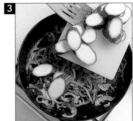

Egg Curry

This curry can be made very quickly. It can either be served as a side dish or with an Indian bread, as a light lunch.

3.5 points

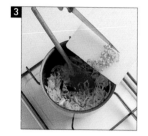

NUTRITIONAL INFORMATION

Calories 207	Protein 9g
Carbohydrate 4g	Sugars 3g
Fat 18g	Saturates 3g

 10 MINS   15 MINS

SERVES 4

INGREDIENTS

4 tbsp oil

1 medium onion, sliced

1 fresh red chilli, finely chopped

½ tsp chilli powder

½ tsp fresh ginger root, finely chopped

½ tsp fresh garlic, crushed

4 medium eggs

1 firm tomato, sliced

fresh coriander (cilantro) leaves

1 Heat the oil in a large saucepan.

2 Add the sliced onion to the pan and fry until just softened and a light golden colour.

3 Add the red chilli, chilli powder, ginger and garlic and stir-fry the mixture, over a low heat, for about 1 minute.

4 Add the eggs and tomatoes to the mixture in the pan and continue cooking, stirring gently to break up the eggs when they begin to cook, for 3–5 minutes.

5 Sprinkle the fresh coriander (cilantro) leaves over the mixture.

6 Transfer the egg curry to serving plates and serve hot with Indian bread, if you wish.

COOK'S TIP

Both the leaves and finely chopped stems of coriander (cilantro) are used in Indian cooking, to flavour dishes and as edible garnishes. It has a very distinctive and pronounced taste.

Tomato Curry

This vegetarian tomato curry is served topped with hard-boiled (hard cooked) eggs and goes well with Spiced Rice & Lentils (see page 49).

3 points

NUTRITIONAL INFORMATION

Calories	175	Protein	6g
Carbohydrate	4g	Sugars	4g
Fat	16g	Saturates	2g

 15 MINS 20 MINS

SERVES 4

INGREDIENTS

400 g/14 oz can tomatoes

1 tsp fresh ginger root, chopped finely

1 tsp fresh garlic, crushed

1 tsp chilli powder

1 tsp salt

½ tsp ground coriander

½ tsp ground cumin

4 tbsp oil

½ tsp onion seeds

½ tsp mustard seeds

½ tsp fenugreek seeds

1 pinch white cumin seeds

3 dried red chillies

2 tbsp lemon juice

3 eggs, hard–boiled (hard–cooked)

fresh coriander (cilantro) leaves

1 Place the tomatoes in a large mixing bowl.

2 Add the ginger, garlic, chilli powder, salt, ground coriander and ground cumin to the tomatoes and blend well.

3 Heat the oil in a saucepan. Add the onion, mustard, fenugreek and white cumin seeds, and the dried red chillies, and stir-fry for about 1 minute. Remove the pan from the heat.

4 Add the tomato mixture to the spicy oil mixture and return to the heat. Stir-fry the mixture for about 3 minutes, then reduce the heat and cook with the lid ajar for 7–10 minutes, stirring occasionally.

5 Sprinkle over the lemon juice sparingly.

6 Transfer the tomato curry to a serving dish, set aside and keep warm until required.

7 Shell and halve the hard–boiled (hard–cooked) eggs, then gently add them, yolk end down, to the tomato curry.

8 Garnish with fresh coriander (cilantro) leaves and serve hot.

COOK'S TIP

This tomato curry can be made in advance and frozen, as it freezes particularly well.

Green Bean & Potato Curry

You can use fresh or canned green beans for this vegetable curry. I would recommend you serve an oil-dressed dhal with this, for a good contrast.

7 points

NUTRITIONAL INFORMATION

Calories	422	Protein	4g
Carbohydrate	18g	Sugars	2g
Fat	38g	Saturates	4g

 15 MINS   30 MINS

SERVES 4

INGREDIENTS

300 ml/½ pint/1¼ cups oil

1 tsp white cumin seeds

1 tsp mustard and onion seeds

4 dried red chillies

3 fresh tomatoes, sliced

1 tsp salt

1 tsp fresh ginger root, finely chopped

1 tsp fresh garlic, crushed

1 tsp chilli powder

200 g/7 oz green cut beans

2 medium potatoes, peeled and diced

300 ml/½ pint/1¼ cups water

fresh coriander (cilantro) leaves, chopped

2 green chillies, finely chopped

1 Heat the oil in a large, heavy-based saucepan.

2 Add the white cumin seeds, mustard and onion seeds and dried red chillies to the saucepan, stirring well.

3 Add the tomato slices to the saucepan and stir-fry the mixture for 3–5 minutes.

4 Mix together the salt, ginger, garlic and chilli powder and spoon into the pan. Blend the whole mixture together.

5 Add the green beans and potatoes to the pan and stir-fry for about 5 minutes.

6 Add the water to the pan, reduce the heat and leave to simmer for 10–15 minutes, stirring occasionally.

7 Garnish the green bean and potato curry with chopped coriander (cilantro) leaves and green chillies and serve hot with cooked rice.

COOK'S TIP

Mustard seeds are often fried in oil or ghee to bring out their flavour before being combined with other ingredients.

Potatoes with Spices & Onions

Masala aloo are potatoes cooked in spices and onions. Semi-dry when cooked, they make an excellent accompaniment to almost any curry.

5 points

NUTRITIONAL INFORMATION

Calories 304	Protein 3g
Carbohydrate ...19g	Sugars 5g
Fat 26g	Saturates 3g

10 MINS   15 MINS

SERVES 4

INGREDIENTS

6 tbsp oil

2 medium-sized onions, chopped finely

1 tsp fresh ginger root, finely chopped

1 tsp fresh garlic, crushed

1 tsp chilli powder

1½ tsp ground cumin

1½ tsp ground coriander

1 tsp salt

400 g/14 oz can new potatoes

1 tbsp lemon juice

BAGHAAR

3 tbsp oil

3 dried red chillies

½ tsp onion seeds

½ tsp mustard seeds

½ tsp fenugreek seeds

TO GARNISH

fresh coriander (cilantro) leaves

1 green chilli, finely chopped

COOK'S TIP

You could also serve these spicy potatoes and onions, for a change, with roast lamb or lamb chops.

1 Heat the oil in a large saucepan. Add the onions and fry, stirring, until golden brown. Reduce the heat, add the ginger, garlic, chilli powder, ground cumin, ground coriander and salt and stir-fry for about 1 minute. Remove the pan from the heat and set aside until required.

2 Drain the water from the potatoes. Add the potatoes to the onion mixture and spice mixture. Sprinkle over the lemon juice and mix well.

3 To make the baghaar, heat some more oil in a separate saucepan. Add the chopped red chillies, onion seeds, mustard seeds and fenugreek seeds and fry, stirring constantly, until the seeds turn a shade darker. Remove the pan from the heat and pour the baghaar over the spicy potato mixture.

4 Garnish with coriander (cilantro) leaves and chillies.

Chickpea Curry

This curry is very popular amongst the many vegetarian people in India and is perhaps the most delicious of the many different ways of cooking chickpeas.

5 points

NUTRITIONAL INFORMATION

Calories 309	Protein 8g
Carbohydrate . . . 28g	Sugars 5g
Fat 19g	Saturates 2g

 15 MINS   20 MINS

SERVES 4

I N G R E D I E N T S

6 tbsp oil

2 medium onions, sliced

1 tsp fresh ginger root, finely chopped

1 tsp ground cumin

1 tsp ground coriander

1 tsp fresh garlic, crushed

1 tsp chilli powder

2 fresh green chillies

fresh coriander (cilantro) leaves

150 ml/¼ pint/⅔ cup water

1 large potato

400 g/14 oz can chickpeas (garbanzo beans), drained

1 tbsp lemon juice

1 Heat the oil in a large saucepan.

2 Add the sliced onions to the pan and fry, stirring occasionally, until golden brown.

3 Reduce the heat, then add the ginger, ground cumin, ground coriander, garlic, chilli powder, chopped fresh green chillies and fresh coriander (cilantro) leaves to the saucepan, stirring the ingredients constantly for about 2 minutes.

4 Add the water to the mixture in the pan and stir to mix.

5 Using a sharp knife, cut the potato into small dice.

6 Add the potatoes and the drained chickpeas (garbanzo beans) to the mixture in the pan, cover and leave to simmer, stirring occasionally, for 5–7 minutes.

7 Sprinkle the lemon juice over the curry.

8 Transfer the chickpea (garbanzo bean) curry to serving dishes. Serve the curry hot with chapati, if you wish.

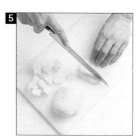

COOK'S TIP

Using canned chickpeas (garbanzo beans) saves time, but you can use dried chickpeas (garbanzo beans) if you prefer. Soak them overnight, then boil them for 15–20 minutes or until soft.

Potatoes & Peas

This quick and easy-to-prepare vegetarian dish can be served either as an accompaniment or on its own with chapatis.

8 points

NUTRITIONAL INFORMATION

Calories 498   Protein 6g
Carbohydrate . . . 35g   Sugars 4g
Fat . . . . 38g   Saturates 4g

🍲 15 MINS   🕐 30 MINS

SERVES 4

INGREDIENTS

150 ml/¼ pint/⅔ cup oil

3 medium onions, sliced

1 tsp fresh garlic, crushed

1 tsp fresh ginger root, finely chopped

1 tsp chilli powder

½ tsp turmeric

1 tsp salt

2 fresh green chillies, finely chopped

300 ml/½ pint/1¼ cups water

3 medium potatoes

100 g/3½ oz peas

fresh coriander (cilantro) leaves, to garnish

chopped red chillies, to garnish

1 Heat the oil in a large frying-pan (skillet). Add the onions to the pan and fry them, stirring occasionally, until they are golden brown.

2 Mix together the garlic, ginger, chilli powder, turmeric, salt and fresh green chillies. Add the spice mixture to the onions in the pan.

3 Stir in 150 ml/¼ pint/⅔ cup of the water, cover and cook until the onions are cooked through.

4 Meanwhile, peel and rinse the potatoes then cut them into six slices each, using a sharp knife.

5 Add the potato slices to the mixture in the pan and stir-fry for 5 minutes.

6 Add the peas and the remaining 150 ml/ ¼ pint/⅔ cup of the water to the pan, cover and cook for 7–10 minutes.

7 Transfer the potatoes and peas to serving plates and serve garnished with fresh coriander (cilantro) leaves.

COOK'S TIP

Turmeric is an aromatic root which is dried and ground to produce the distinctive bright yellow–orange powder used in many Indian dishes. It has a warm, aromatic smell and a full, somewhat musty taste.

Potato & Cauliflower Curry

Potatoes and cauliflower go very well together. Served with a dhal and Pooris (see page 51), this dish makes a perfect vegetarian meal.

8 points

NUTRITIONAL INFORMATION

Calories 487	Protein 6g	
Carbohydrate ... 31g	Sugars 7g	
Fat 39g	Saturates 4g	

 15 MINS   25 MINS

SERVES 4

I N G R E D I E N T S

150 ml/¼ pint/⅔ cup oil

½ tsp white cumin seeds

4 dried red chillies

2 medium onions, sliced

1 tsp fresh ginger root, finely chopped

1 tsp fresh garlic, crushed

1 tsp chilli powder

1 tsp salt

1 pinch of turmeric

3 medium potatoes, peeled and sliced

½ cauliflower, cut into small florets

2 green chillies (optional)

fresh coriander (cilantro) leaves

150 ml/¼ pint/⅔ cup water

COOK'S TIP

Always handle chillies with caution, preferably wearing rubber gloves because the juices are extremely pungent. Wash your hands thoroughly after preparing and handling chillies and do not allow your fingers near your eyes as this can be very painful.

1 Heat the oil in a large saucepan.

2 Add the white cumin seeds and dried red chillies to the pan, stirring to mix.

3 Add the sliced onions to the pan and fry, stirring occasionally, until golden brown.

4 Mix the ginger, garlic, chilli powder, salt and turmeric together in a separate bowl then add the spice mixture to the onions and stir-fry for about 2 minutes.

5 Add the peeled and sliced potatoes and the cauliflower florets to the onion and spice mixture, stirring thoroughly to coat all the vegetables in the spice mixture.

6 Reduce the heat and add the green chillies (if using), fresh coriander (cilantro) leaves and water to the pan. Cover and leave the mixture to simmer for about 10–15 minutes.

7 Transfer the potato and cauliflower curry to warm serving plates and serve immediately.

Onion Dhal

This dhal is semi-dry when cooked so it is best to serve it with a curry which has a sauce. Use ordinary onions if spring onions (scallions) are unavailable.

4 points

NUTRITIONAL INFORMATION

Calories 236	Protein 7g	
Carbohydrate ... 15g	Sugars 1g	
Fat 17g	Saturates 2g	

 10 MINS   35 MINS

SERVES 4

INGREDIENTS

100 g/3½ oz/½ cup masoor dhal

6 tbsp oil

1 small bunch spring onions (scallions), trimmed and chopped, including the green part

1 tsp fresh ginger root, finely chopped

1 tsp fresh garlic, crushed

½ tsp chilli powder

½ tsp turmeric

300 ml/½ pint/1¼ cups water

1 tsp salt

1 fresh green chilli, finely chopped

fresh coriander (cilantro) leaves

1 Rinse the masoor dhal lentils and set aside until required.

2 Heat the oil in a saucepan. Add the chopped spring onions (scallions) to the pan and fry, stirring constantly, until lightly browned.

3 Reduce the heat and add the ginger, garlic, chilli powder and turmeric to the pan. Stir-fry the spring onions (scallions) with the spices.

4 Add the lentils and mix to blend together.

5 Add the water to the lentil mixture in the pan, reduce the heat further and cook for 20–25 minutes.

6 When the lentils are cooked thoroughly, add the salt and stir with a wooden spoon to gently combine.

7 Garnish the onion lentils with the chopped green chillies and fresh coriander (cilantro) leaves. Transfer the onion lentils to a serving dish and serve immediately.

COOK'S TIP

Masoor dhal are small, round, pale orange split lentils. They turn a pale yellow colour when cooked.

Spiced Rice & Lentils

This is a lovely combination of rice and masoor dhal, simple to cook and delicious served with minced lamb and chutney.

4·5 points

NUTRITIONAL INFORMATION

Calories 279	Protein 7g
Carbohydrate . . . 49g	Sugars 1g
Fat 6g	Saturates 3g

 10 MINS   30 MINS

SERVES 4

INGREDIENTS

200 g/7 oz/1 cup basmati rice

175 g/6 oz/¾ cup masoor dhal

2 tbsp pure or vegetable ghee

1 small onion, sliced

1 tsp fresh ginger root, finely chopped

1 tsp fresh garlic, crushed

½ tsp turmeric

600 ml/1 pint/2½ cups water

1 tsp salt

1 Combine the rice and dhal and rinse twice, rubbing with your fingers, and removing any stones. Set aside until required.

2 Heat the ghee in a large saucepan. Add the onion and fry, stirring occasionally, for about 2 minutes.

3 Reduce the heat, add the ginger, garlic, and turmeric and stir-fry for 1 minute.

4 Add the rice and dhal to the mixture in the pan and mix gently.

5 Add the water to the mixture in the pan and bring to the boil. Reduce the heat and cook, covered, for 20–25 minutes.

6 Just before serving, add the salt and mix well to combine.

7 Transfer the spiced rice and lentils to a serving dish and serve immediately.

COOK'S TIP

Many Indian recipes specify using ghee as the cooking fat. This is because it is similar to clarified butter in that it can be heated to a very high temperature without burning. Ghee adds a nutty flavour to dishes and a glossy shine to sauces. You can buy ghee in cans, and a vegetarian version is also available. Store at room temperature or keep in the refrigerator.

Lamb Biryani

Cooked on festive occasions, especially for weddings, lamb biryani is amongst the most popular dishes in India.

NUTRITIONAL INFORMATION

Calories 985	Protein 65g	
Carbohydrate ... 99g	Sugars 8g	
Fat 37g	Saturates 17g	

15 MINS   1 HR 10 MINS

SERVES 4

INGREDIENTS

150 ml/¼ pint/⅔ cup milk

1 tsp saffron

5 tbsp ghee

3 medium onions, sliced

1 kg/2 lb 5 oz lean lamb, cubed

7 tbsp natural yogurt

1½ tsp fresh ginger root, finely chopped

1½ tsp fresh garlic, crushed

2 tsp garam masala

2 tsp salt

¼ tsp turmeric

600 ml/1 pint/2½ cups water

450 g/1 lb/2¼ cups basmati rice

2 tsp black cumin seeds

3 cardamoms

4 tbsp lemon juice

2 fresh green chillies

¼ bunch fresh coriander (cilantro) leaves

1   Boil the milk in a pan with the saffron and set aside. Heat the ghee in a pan and fry the onions until golden. Remove half of the onions and ghee from the pan and set aside.

2   Combine the meat, yogurt, ginger, garlic, garam masala, 1 tsp salt and turmeric in a large bowl.

3   Return the pan with the ghee and onions to the heat, add the meat mixture, stir for 3 minutes and add the water. Cook on a low heat for 45 minutes, stirring occasionally. If the meat is not tender, add 150 ml/¼ pint/⅔ cup water and cook for 15 minutes. Once the water has evaporated, stir-fry for 2 minutes and set aside.

4   Meanwhile, place the rice in a pan. Add the cumin seeds, cardamoms, salt and enough water for cooking, and cook over a medium heat until the rice is half-cooked. Drain. Remove half of the rice.

5   Spoon the meat mixture on top of the rice in the pan. Add half each of the saffron milk, lemon juice, chillies and coriander (cilantro). Add the reserved onion and ghee mixture, the other half of the rice and other ingredients. Cover and cook over a low heat for 15–20 minutes. Serve hot.

Poori

This bread is served mostly with vegetarian meals and particularly with Potato Curry (see page 36). Pooris are deep-fried, but they are very light.

4 points

NUTRITIONAL INFORMATION

Calories 169	Protein 3g
Carbohydrate . . . 14g	Sugars 0g
Fat 11g	Saturates 6g

 30 MINS   15 MINS

SERVES 10

INGREDIENTS

225 g/8 oz/1½ cups wholemeal flour (ata or chapati flour)

½ tsp salt

150 ml/¼ pint/⅔ cup water

600 ml/1 pint/2½ cups oil

1 Place the flour and salt in a large mixing bowl and stir to combine.

2 Make a well in the centre of the flour. Gradually pour in the water and mix together to form a dough, adding more water if necessary.

3 Knead the dough until it is smooth and elastic and leave in a warm place to rise for 15 minutes.

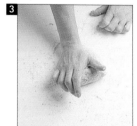

COOK'S TIP

You can make pooris in advance, if you prefer. Wrap in kitchen foil and reheat in a hot oven for about 10 minutes when required.

4 Divide the dough into about 10 equal portions and with lightly oiled or floured hands pat each into a smooth ball.

5 On a lightly oiled or floured surface, roll out each dough ball to form a thin round.

6 Heat the oil in a deep frying-pan (skillet). Deep-fry the rounds in batches, turning once, until golden in colour.

7 Remove the pooris from the pan and drain. Serve hot.

Black-Eye Beans

This is semi-dry when cooked, and is very good served with a few drops of lemon juice or with chapatis and a wet curry.

13.5 pants

NUTRITIONAL INFORMATION

Calories 807	Protein 11g
Carbohydrate . . . 22g	Sugars 5g
Fat 76g	Saturates 8g

 15 MINS 45 MINS

SERVES 4

I N G R E D I E N T S

150 g/5½ oz/1 cup black-eye beans (peas)

300 ml/½ pint/1¼ cups oil

2 medium onions, sliced

1 tsp fresh ginger root, finely chopped

1 tsp fresh garlic, crushed

1 tsp chilli powder

1½ tsp salt

1½ tsp ground coriander

1½ tsp ground cumin

150 ml/¼ pint/⅔ cup water

2 green chillies

fresh coriander (cilantro) leaves

1 tbsp lemon juice

COOK'S TIP

Black-eye beans (peas) are oval-shaped, grey or beige beans (peas) with a dark dot in the centre. They have a slightly smoky flavour. They are sold canned as well as dried. Black-eye beans should be soaked overnight before use.

1 Rinse and soak the black-eye beans (peas) in a bowl of water overnight.

2 Place the black-eye beans (peas) in a pan of water and bring to a boil over a low heat for about 30 minutes. Drain the beans (peas) thoroughly and set aside.

3 Heat the oil in a pan. Add the onions and fry until golden brown. Add the ginger, garlic, chilli powder, salt, ground coriander and ground cumin and stir-fry the mixture for 3–5 minutes.

4 Add the water to the pan, cover and cook the mixture until all of the water has completely evaporated.

5 Add the boiled black-eye beans (peas), green chillies and coriander (cilantro) leaves to the onions and stir to blend together. Stir-fry the bean (pea) mixture for 3–5 minutes.

6 Transfer the black-eye beans (peas) to a serving dish and sprinkle over the lemon juice. Serve hot or cold.

Pulao Rice

Plain boiled rice is eaten by most people in India every day, but for entertaining we tend to choose this as a more interesting rice dish.

8 points

NUTRITIONAL INFORMATION

Calories 459	Protein 8g	
Carbohydrate ... 80g	Sugars 0g	
Fat 12g	Saturates 5g	

 5 MINS 25 MINS

SERVES 2

INGREDIENTS

200 g/7 oz/1 cup basmati rice

2 tbsp ghee

3 green cardamoms

2 cloves

3 peppercorns

½ tsp salt

½ tsp saffron

400 ml/¾ pint/2 cups water

1 Rinse the rice twice and set aside in a bowl until required.

2 Heat the ghee in a saucepan. Add the cardamoms, cloves and peppercorns to the pan and fry, stirring, for about 1 minute.

3 Add the rice and stir-fry for a further 2 minutes.

4 Add the salt, saffron and water to the rice mixture and reduce the heat. Cover the pan and leave to simmer over a low heat until the water has evaporated.

5 Transfer to a serving dish and serve hot.

COOK'S TIP

The most expensive of all spices, saffron strands are the stamens of a type of crocus. They give dishes a rich, golden colour, as well as adding a distinctive, slightly bitter taste. Saffron is sold as a powder or in strands. Saffron strands are more expensive, but do have a superior flavour. Some books recommend substituting turmeric – although the colours are similar, the tastes are not.

Tomato Rice

Rice with tomatoes and onions adds colour to your table when garnished with green chillies, coriander (cilantro) leaves and eggs.

13.5 points

NUTRITIONAL INFORMATION

Calories 842	Protein 15g
Carbohydrate . . . 99g	Sugars 7g
Fat 43g	Saturates 5g

🍲 10 MINS   🕐 35 MINS

SERVES 4

I N G R E D I E N T S

150 ml/¼ pint/⅔ cup oil

2 medium onions, sliced

1 tsp onion seeds

1 tsp fresh ginger root, finely chopped

1 tsp fresh garlic, crushed

½ tsp turmeric

1 tsp chilli powder

1½ tsp salt

400 g/14 oz can tomatoes

450 g/1 lb/2¼ cups basmati rice

600 ml/1 pint/2½ cups water

T O   G A R N I S H

3 fresh green chillies, finely chopped

fresh coriander (cilantro) leaves, chopped

3 hard–boiled (hard–cooked) eggs

1 Heat the oil in a saucepan and fry the onions until golden brown.

2 Add the onion seeds, ginger, garlic, turmeric, chilli powder and salt, stirring to combine.

3 Reduce the heat, add the tomatoes and stir-fry for 10 minutes.

4 Add the rice to the tomato mixture, stirring gently, to coat the rice in the mixture.

5 Pour in the water, stirring to incorporate. Cover the pan and cook over a low heat until the water has been absorbed and the rice is cooked.

6 Transfer the tomato rice to a serving dish.

7 Garnish with the finely chopped green chillies, fresh coriander (cilantro) leaves and halved hard–boiled (hard–cooked) eggs. Serve the tomato rice dish immediately.

COOK'S TIP

Onion seeds are always used whole in Indian cooking. They are often used in pickles and often sprinkled over the top of Naan Breads (see page 55). Ironically, onion seeds don't have anything to do with the vegetable, but they look similar to the plant's seed, hence the name.

Naan Bread

There are many ways of making naan bread, but this recipe is very easy to follow. Naan bread should preferably be served warm.

4.5 points

NUTRITIONAL INFORMATION

Calories 203	Protein 3g
Carbohydrate ... 27g	Sugars 2g
Fat 10g	Saturates 6g

2 HOURS   10 MINS

SERVES 6

INGREDIENTS

1 tsp sugar

1 tsp fresh yeast

150 ml/¼ pint/⅔ cup warm water

200 g/7 oz/1½ cups plain (all–purpose) flour

1 tbsp ghee

1 tsp salt

50 g/1¾ oz/6 tbsp unsalted butter

1 tsp poppy seeds

1 Put the sugar and yeast in a small bowl or jug with the warm water and mix well until the yeast has dissolved. Set aside for about 10 minutes or until the mixture is frothy.

2 Place the flour in a large mixing bowl. Make a well in the middle of the flour, add the ghee and salt and pour in the yeast mixture. Mix well to form a dough, using your hands and adding more water if required.

3 Turn the dough out on to a floured surface and knead for 5 minutes or until smooth.

4 Return the dough to the bowl, cover and leave to rise in a warm place for 1½ hours or until doubled in size.

5 Turn the dough out on to a floured surface and knead for a further 2 minutes. Break off small balls with your hand and pat them into rounds about 12 cm/5 inches in diameter and 1 cm/½ inch thick.

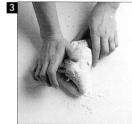

6 Place the dough rounds on to a greased sheet of foil and grill (broil) under a very hot pre-heated grill (broiler) for 7–10 minutes, turning twice and brushing with the butter and sprinkling with the poppy seeds.

7 Serve warm immediately, or keep wrapped in foil until required.

Spinach & Chana Dhal

This makes a good vegetarian accompaniment to almost any meal. For a contrast in colour and taste, cook with a Tomato Curry (see page 42).

3·5 points

NUTRITIONAL INFORMATION

Calories 220	Protein 7g
Carbohydrate ... 10g	Sugars 1g
Fat 18g	Saturates 2g

 15 MINS   45 MINS

SERVES 4

I N G R E D I E N T S

4 tbsp chana dhal

6 tbsp oil

1 tsp mixed onion and mustard seeds

4 dried red chillies

400–450 g/14–16 oz can spinach, drained

1 tsp fresh ginger root, chopped finely

1 tsp ground coriander

1 tsp ground cumin

1 tsp salt

1 tsp chilli powder

2 tbsp lemon juice

1 green chilli, to garnish

COOK'S TIP

Very similar in appearance to moong dhal – the yellow split peas – chana dhal has slightly less shiny grains. It is used as a binding agent and may be bought from Indian and Pakistani grocers.

1 Soak the chana dhal in a bowl of warm water for at least 3 hours, preferably overnight.

2 Drain the lentils then place them in a saucepan, cover with water, bring to the boil and cook for 30 minutes.

3 Heat the oil in another smaller saucepan. Add the mixed onion and mustard seeds and the dried red chillies and fry them, stirring constantly, until the mixed seeds turn a shade darker.

4 Add the drained spinach to the pan, mixing gently.

5 Add the ginger, ground coriander, ground cumin, salt and chilli powder to the mixture in the pan. Reduce the heat and gently stir-fry the mixture for about 7–10 minutes.

6 Add the lentils to the saucepan and blend well into the spicy spinach mixture to combine, stirring gently so that it does not break up.

7 Transfer the mixture to a serving dish. Sprinkle over the lemon juice and garnish with the green chilli. Serve immediately.

Brown Rice with Fruit & Nuts

Here is a tasty and filling rice dish that is nice and spicy and includes fruits for a refreshing flavour and toasted nuts for an interesting crunchy texture.

11.5 points

NUTRITIONAL INFORMATION

Calories 649   Protein 16g
Carbohydrate . . . 98g   Sugars 32g
Fat . . . . 25g   Saturates 8g

15 MINS   1 HOUR

SERVES 4

I N G R E D I E N T S

4 tbsp vegetable ghee or oil

1 large onion, chopped

2 garlic cloves, crushed

2.5 cm/1 inch ginger root, chopped finely

1 tsp chilli powder

1 tsp cumin seeds

1 tbsp mild or medium curry powder or paste

300 g/10 oz/1½ cups brown rice

850 ml/1½ pints/3½ cups boiling vegetable stock

400 g/14 oz can chopped tomatoes

175 g/6 oz ready-soaked dried apricots or peaches, cut into slivers

1 red (bell) pepper, cored, seeded and diced

90 g/3 oz frozen peas

1–2 small, slightly green bananas

60–90 g/2–3oz/⅓–½ cup toasted mixed nuts

salt and pepper

1 Heat the ghee or oil in a large saucepan, add the onion and fry gently for 3 minutes.

2 Stir in the garlic, ginger, chilli powder, cumin seeds, curry powder or paste and rice. Cook gently for 2 minutes, stirring, until the rice is coated in the spiced oil.

3 Pour in the boiling stock, stirring to mix. Add the tomatoes and season with salt and pepper. Bring to the boil, then reduce the heat, cover and leave to simmer gently for 40 minutes or until the rice is almost cooked and most of the liquid is absorbed.

4 Add the apricots or peaches, red (bell) pepper and peas to the rice mixture in the pan. Cover and continue cooking for 10 minutes.

5 Remove the pan from the heat and leave to stand for 5 minutes without uncovering.

6 Peel and slice the bananas. Uncover the rice mixture and toss with a fork to mix. Add the toasted nuts and sliced banana and toss lightly.

7 Transfer the rice dish to a serving platter and serve hot.

Gram Flour Bread

This filling bread is not eaten on a regular basis but is cooked occasionally. It is best served with any vegetarian curry and lime pickle.

2.5 points

NUTRITIONAL INFORMATION

Calories 165   Protein 7g
Carbohydrate . . . 27g   Sugars 2g
Fat . . . . 4g   Saturates 1g

 30 MINS   15 MINS

SERVES 4

I N G R E D I E N T S

100 g/3½ oz/¾ cup wholemeal flour (ata or chapati flour)

75 g/2¾ oz/½ cup gram flour

½ tsp salt

1 small onion

fresh coriander (cilantro) leaves, chopped very finely

2 fresh green chillies, chopped very finely

150 ml/¼ pint/⅔ cup water

2 tsp ghee

1 Sift the wholemeal and gram flours together in a large mixing bowl. Add the salt to the flour and mix to combine.

2 Using a sharp knife, peel and chop the onion very finely.

3 Blend the onion, chopped coriander (cilantro) and chillies into the flour mixture.

4 Add the water and mix to form a soft dough. Cover the dough and set aside for about 15 minutes.

5 Knead the dough for 5–7 minutes.

6 Divide the dough into 8 equal portions.

7 Roll out the dough portions to about 18 cm/7 inches on a lightly floured surface.

8 Place the dough portions individually in a frying-pan (skillet) and cook over a medium heat, turning three times and lightly greasing each side with the ghee each time. Transfer the gram flour bread to serving plates and serve hot.

COOK'S TIP

Also called besan flour, gram flour is a pale yellow flour made from ground chickpeas (garbanzo beans). In Indian kitchens it is used to make breads, bhajis and batters and to thicken sauces and stabilize yogurt when it is added to hot dishes. Buy it from Indian food stores or large health food stores and store in a cool, dark place in an air-tight container.

Chickpea Snack

Fresh chickpeas (garbanzo beans) must be soaked overnight but canned alternatives can be used without sacrificing much of the flavour.

6 points

NUTRITIONAL INFORMATION

Calories . . . . 408 Protein 17g
Carbohydrate . . . 77g Sugars 23g
Fat . . . . 6g Saturates 1g

 10 MINS   10 MINS

SERVES 2

I N G R E D I E N T S

400 g/14 oz can chickpeas (garbanzo beans), drained

2 medium potatoes

1 medium onion

2 tbsp tamarind paste

6 tbsp water

1 tsp chilli powder

2 tsp sugar

1 tsp salt

T O   G A R N I S H

1 tomato, sliced

2 fresh green chillies, chopped

fresh coriander (cilantro) leaves

1 Place the drained chickpeas (garbanzo beans) in a bowl.

2 Using a sharp knife, dice the potatoes.

3 Place the diced potatoes in a saucepan of water and boil until cooked through. Test by inserting the tip of a knife into the potatoes – they should feel soft and tender. Set aside until required.

4 Using a sharp knife, finely chop the onion. Set aside until required.

5 Mix together the tamarind paste and water in a small mixing bowl.

6 Add the chilli powder, sugar and salt to the tamarind paste mixture and mix together. Pour the mixture over the chickpeas (garbanzo beans).

7 Add the onion and the diced potatoes, and stir to mix. Season to taste with a little salt.

8 Transfer to a serving bowl and garnish with tomatoes, chillies and coriander (cilantro) leaves.

COOK'S TIP

Cream-coloured and resembling a hazelnut in appearance, chickpeas (garbanzo breans) have a nutty flavour and slightly crunchy texture. Indian cooks also grind these to make a flour called gram or besan, which is used to make breads, thicken sauces, and to make batters for deep-fried dishes.

Sweet & Sour Fruit

This mixture of fresh and canned fruit, which has a sweet and sour flavour, is very cooling, especially in the summer.

2.5 points

NUTRITIONAL INFORMATION

Calories 166	Protein 2g	
Carbohydrate . . . 42g	Sugars 40g	
Fat 0g	Saturates 0g	

10 MINS   0 MINS

SERVES 4

INGREDIENTS

400 g/14 oz can mixed fruit cocktail

400 g/14 oz can guavas

2 large bananas

3 apples

1 tsp ground black pepper

1 tsp salt

2 tbsp lemon juice

½ tsp ground ginger

fresh mint leaves, to garnish

1 Drain the can of fruit cocktail and pour the fruit pieces into a deep mixing bowl.

2 Mix the guavas and their syrup with the drained fruit cocktail.

3 Peel the bananas and cut into slices.

4 Peel and core the apples (optional) and cut into dice.

5 Add the pieces of fresh fruit to the bowl containing the canned fruit and mix together.

6 Add the ground black pepper, salt, lemon juice and ginger and stir well to mix.

7 Serve as a snack garnished with a few fresh mint leaves.

COOK'S TIP

Ginger is one of the most popular spices in India and also one of the oldest. It can be bought as fresh ginger root in most large supermarkets. It should always be peeled before use and can be finely chopped or puréed. Ground ginger is also useful to have in your storecupboard.

Chickpea Salad

This attractive-looking salad can be served with a couple of kebabs (kabobs) for a delicious light lunch or an informal supper.

2 points

NUTRITIONAL INFORMATION

Calories 150   Protein 8g
Carbohydrate . . . 24g   Sugars 11g
Fat . . . . 3g   Saturates 0g

 10 MINS   0 MINS

SERVES 4

INGREDIENTS

400 g/14 oz can chickpeas (garbanzo beans)

4 carrots

1 bunch spring onions (scallions)

1 medium cucumber

½ tsp salt

½ tsp pepper

3 tbsp lemon juice

1 red (bell) pepper, sliced

3 Cut the spring onions (scallions) into small, even pieces.

4 Cut the cucumber into thick quarters.

5 Add the sliced carrots, spring onions (scallions) and cucumber to the chickpeas (garbanzo beans) and mix.

6 Season with the salt and pepper and sprinkle with the lemon juice.

7 Toss the salad ingredients together gently in the bowl using 2 serving spoons.

8 Using a sharp knife, slice the red (bell) pepper thinly.

9 Arrange the slices of red (bell) pepper on top of the chickpea (garbanzo bean) salad. Serve the salad immediately or leave to chill in the refrigerator and serve when required.

1 Drain the chickpeas (garbanzo beans) and pour them into a large salad bowl.

2 Using a sharp knife, peel and slice the carrots.

COOK'S TIP

Using canned chickpeas (garbanzo beans) rather than the dried ones speeds up the cooking time.

Spicy Corn

This dish is an ideal accompaniment to a wide range of Indian meals.

4 points

NUTRITIONAL INFORMATION

Calories	163	Protein	3g
Carbohydrate	17g	Sugars	7g
Fat	10g	Saturates	6g

 10 MINS   15 MINS

SERVES 4

INGREDIENTS

200 g/7 oz/1 cup canned or frozen sweetcorn

1 tsp ground cumin

1 tsp fresh garlic, crushed

1 tsp ground coriander

1 tsp salt

2 fresh green chillies

1 medium onion, finely chopped

3 tbsp unsalted butter

4 red chillies, crushed

½ tsp lemon juice

fresh coriander (cilantro) leaves

1 Thaw frozen sweetcorn or drain canned sweetcorn and set aside.

2 Place the ground cumin, garlic, ground coriander, salt, 1 fresh green chilli and the onion in a pestle and mortar or a food processor and grind to form a smooth paste.

3 Heat the butter in a large frying pan (skillet). Add the onion and spice mixture to the pan and fry over a medium heat, stirring occasionally, for about 5–7 minutes.

4 Add the crushed red chillies to the pan and stir to mix.

5 Add the sweetcorn to the pan and stir-fry for a further 2 minutes.

6 Add the remaining green chilli, lemon juice and the fresh coriander (cilantro) leaves to the pan, stirring occasionally to combine.

7 Transfer to a warm serving dish. Garnish with fresh coriander (cilantro) and serve hot.

COOK'S TIP

Coriander is available ground or as seeds and is one of the essential ingredients in Indian cooking. Coriander seeds are often dry roasted before use to develop their flavour.

Spiced Semolina

A south Indian savoury snack which is very quick and easy to prepare, this aromatic dish should be served warm.

8·5 points

NUTRITIONAL INFORMATION

Calories	509	Protein	6g
Carbohydrate	24g	Sugars	1g
Fat	44g	Saturates	5g

 10 MINS   20 MINS

SERVES 4

I N G R E D I E N T S

150 ml/¼ pint/⅔ cup oil

1 tsp mixed onion and mustard seeds

4 dried red chillies

4 curry leaves (fresh or dried)

8 tbsp coarse semolina

50 g/1¾ oz cashew nuts

1 tsp salt

150 ml/¼ pint/⅔ cup water

1 Heat the oil in a large, heavy frying-pan (skillet).

2 Add the mixed onion and mustard seeds, dried red chillies and curry leaves and stir-fry for about 1 minute, stirring constantly.

3 Reduce the heat and add the coarse semolina and the cashew nuts to the mixture in the pan. Quickly stir-fry for about 5 minutes, moving the mixture around all the time so that it does not catch and burn on the bottom of the pan.

4 Add the salt to the mixture and continue to stir-fry, stirring constantly.

5 Add the water and cook, stirring continuously, until the mixture starts to thicken.

6 Serve the spiced semolina warm as a teatime snack.

COOK'S TIP

Curry leaves are very similar in appearance to bay leaves but are very different in flavour. They can be bought both fresh and dried. They are mainly used to flavour lentil dishes and vegetable curries.

Cool Cucumber Salad

This cooling salad is another good foil for a highly spiced meal. Omit the green chilli, if preferred.

No point

NUTRITIONAL INFORMATION

Calories 13	Protein 1g
Carbohydrate 3g	Sugars 3g
Fat 0g	Saturates 0g

10 MINS   0 MINS

SERVES 4

INGREDIENTS

225 g/8 oz cucumber

1 green chilli (optional)

fresh coriander (cilantro) leaves, finely chopped

2 tbsp lemon juice

½ tsp salt

1 tsp sugar

fresh mint leaves and red (bell) pepper strips, to garnish

1 Using a sharp knife, slice the cucumber thinly. Arrange the cucumber slices on a round serving plate.

2 Using a sharp knife, chop the green chilli (if using).

3 Scatter the chopped chilli over the cucumber.

4 To make the dressing, place the chopped coriander (cilantro) leaves, lemon juice, salt and sugar into a bowl, mix together and set aside.

5 Place the cucumber in the refrigerator and leave to chill for at least 1 hour, or until required.

6 Transfer the cucumber to a serving dish.

7 Pour the dressing over the cucumber just before serving and garnish with fresh mint leaves.

COOK'S TIP

Much of the heat in Indian dishes comes from fresh green chillies, although dried and ground red chillies are also commonplace. In southern India, with its searingly hot temperatures, large quantities of chillies are used because they cause the body to perspire, which has a cooling effect. As a general rule, the smaller the chilli, the hotter it will be.

Mango Chutney

This chutney is particularly good served with a Mint Raita (see page 69).
It is best made well in advance and stored for at least 2 weeks before use.

10.5 points

NUTRITIONAL INFORMATION

Calories 732   Protein 4g
Carbohydrate . . 185g   Sugars 183g
Fat . . . . 1g   Saturates 0g

15 MINS   1¼ HOURS

SERVES 4

INGREDIENTS

1 kg/2 lb 4 oz raw mangoes

4 tbsp salt

600 ml/1 pint/2½ cups water

450 g/1 lb/2⅓ cups sugar

450 ml/¾ pint/2 cups vinegar

2 tsp fresh ginger root, finely chopped

2 tsp fresh garlic, crushed

2 tsp chilli powder

2 cinnamon sticks

75 g/2¾ oz/½ cup raisins

100 g/3½ oz/½ cup dates, stoned

1 Using a sharp knife, peel, halve and stone the mangoes. Cut the mango flesh into cubes. Place the mango in a large bowl. Add the salt and water and leave overnight. Drain the liquid from the mangoes and set aside.

2 Bring the sugar and vinegar to the boil in a large saucepan over a low heat, stirring.

3 Gradually add the mango cubes, stirring to coat the mango in the sugar and vinegar mixture.

4 Add the ginger, garlic, chilli powder, cinnamon sticks, raisins and the dates, and bring to the boil again, stirring

occasionally. Reduce the heat and cook for about 1 hour or until the mixture thickens. Remove from the heat and leave to cool.

5 Remove the cinnamon sticks and discard.

6 Spoon the chutney into clean dry jars and cover tightly with lids. Leave in a cool place for the flavours to fully develop.

COOK'S TIP

When choosing mangoes, select ones that are shiny with unblemished skins. To test if they are ripe, cup the mango in your hand and squeeze it gently – it should give slightly to the touch if ready for eating.

Fried Aubergines in Yogurt

This makes a good alternative to a Raita (see page 69). The aubergines (eggplants) are fried until crisp, then given a baghaar, or seasoned oil dressing.

6.5 points

NUTRITIONAL INFORMATION

Calories	380	Protein	4g
Carbohydrate	6g	Sugars	6g
Fat	38g	Saturates	4g

🍲

⏱ 10 MINS   ⏰ 15 MINS

SERVES 4

I N G R E D I E N T S

200 ml/7 fl oz/¾ cup natural yogurt

75 ml/3 fl oz/⅓ cup water

1 tsp salt

1 medium aubergine (eggplant)

150 ml/¼ pint/⅔ cup oil

1 tsp white cumin seeds

6 dried red chillies

1 Place the yogurt in a bowl and whip with a fork.

2 Add the water and salt to the yogurt and mix together well. Transfer to a serving bowl.

3 Using a sharp knife, slice the aubergine (eggplant) thinly.

COOK'S TIP

Rich in protein and calcium, yogurt plays an important part in Indian cooking. It is used as a marinade, as a creamy flavouring in curries and sauces and as a cooling accompaniment to hot dishes.

4 Heat the oil in a large frying-pan (skillet). Add the aubergine (eggplant) slices and fry, in batches, over a medium heat, turning occasionally, until they begin to turn crisp. Remove from the pan, transfer to a serving plate and keep warm.

5 When all of the aubergine (eggplant) slices have been fried, lower the heat, and add the white cumin seeds and the dried red chillies to the pan. Cook for 1 minute, stirring.

6 Spoon the yogurt on top of the aubergines (eggplants), then pour over the white cumin and red chilli mixture. Serve immediately.

Indian-Style Omelette

Omelettes are very versatile: they go with almost anything and you can serve them at any time of the day.

5·5 points

NUTRITIONAL INFORMATION

Calories 292   Protein 16g
Carbohydrate . . . . 2g   Sugars 5g
Fat . . . . 24g   Saturates 5g

 10 MINS   15 MINS

SERVES 2

I N G R E D I E N T S

1 small onion, very finely chopped

2 green chillies, finely chopped

fresh coriander (cilantro) leaves, finely chopped

4 medium eggs

1 tsp salt

2 tbsp oil

1 Place the onion, chillies and coriander (cilantro) in a large mixing bowl. Mix together, ideally with your fingers.

2 Place the eggs in a separate bowl and whisk together.

3 Add the onion mixture to the eggs and mix together well.

4 Add the salt to the egg and onion mixture and whisk together well.

5 Heat 1 tbsp of the oil in a large frying pan (skillet). Place a ladleful of the omelette batter into the heated pan.

6 Fry the omelette, turning once and pressing down with a flat spoon to make sure that the egg is cooked right through, until the omelette is a golden brown colour.

7 Repeat the same process for the remaining batter. Set the omelettes aside and keep warm while you make the remaining batches of omelettes.

8 Serve the omelettes immediately with paratas or toasted bread. Alternatively, simply serve the omelettes with a crisp green salad for a light lunch.

COOK'S TIP

Indian cooks use a variety of vegetable oils, and groundnut or sunflower oils make good alternatives for most dishes, although sometimes more specialist ones, such as coconut oil, mustard oil and sesame oil, are called for.

Hot Salad

This quickly-made dish is ideal for a cold winter's night.

3 points

NUTRITIONAL INFORMATION

Calories	128	Protein	4g
Carbohydrate	13g	Sugars	12g
Fat	7g	Saturates	4g

10 MINS   15 MINS

SERVES 4

I N G R E D I E N T S

½ medium-sized cauliflower

1 green (bell) pepper

1 red (bell) pepper

½ cucumber

4 carrots

2 tbsp butter

salt and pepper

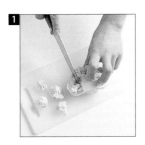

1 Rinse the cauliflower and cut into small florets, using a sharp knife.

2 Cut the (bell) peppers into thin slices.

3 Cut the cucumber into thin slices.

VARIATION

You can replace the vegetables in this recipe with those of your choice, if you prefer.

4 Peel the carrots and cut them into thin slices.

5 Melt the butter in a large saucepan, stirring constantly so that it doesn't burn.

6 Add the cauliflower, (bell) peppers, cucumber and carrots and stir-fry for

5–7 minutes. Season with salt and pepper to taste, cover the pan with a lid, reduce the heat and leave to simmer for about 3 minutes.

7 Transfer the vegetables to a serving dish, toss to mix, and serve immediately.

Raitas

Raitas are very easy to prepare, very versatile and have a cooling effect. The nutritional value is for all three Raitas.

2 points

NUTRITIONAL INFORMATION

Calories	139	Protein	11g
Carbohydrate	21g	Sugars	19g
Fat	2g	Saturates	1g

 20 MINS 0 MINS

SERVES 4

I N G R E D I E N T S

MINT RAITA

200 ml/7 fl oz/¾ cup natural yogurt

50 ml/2 fl oz/4 tbsp water

1 small onion, finely chopped

½ tsp mint sauce

½ tsp salt

3 fresh mint leaves, to garnish

CUCUMBER RAITA

225 g/8 oz cucumber

1 medium onion

½ tsp salt

½ tsp mint sauce

300 ml/10 fl oz/1¼ cups yogurt

150 ml/¼ pint/⅔ cup water

fresh mint leaves, to garnish

AUBERGINE (EGGPLANT) RAITA

1 medium aubergine (eggplant)

1 tsp salt

1 small onion, finely chopped

2 green chillies, finely chopped

200 ml/7 fl oz/¾ cup natural yogurt

3 tbsp water

1 To make the mint raita, place the yogurt in a bowl and whisk with a fork. Gradually add the water, whisking well. Add the onion, mint sauce and salt and blend together. Garnish with the fresh mint leaves.

2 To make the cucumber raita, peel and slice the cucumber. Using a sharp knife, chop the onion finely. Place the cucumber and onion in a large bowl, then add the salt and the mint sauce. Add the yogurt and the water and place the mixture in a liquidizer and blend well. Transfer to a serving bowl and serve garnished with a few fresh mint leaves.

3 To make the aubergine (eggplant) raita, rinse the aubergine (eggplant) and remove the top end. Discard the top and chop the rest into small pieces. Boil the pieces in a pan of water until soft. Drain and mash. Transfer to a serving bowl and add the salt, the onion and green chillies, mixing well. Whip the yogurt with the water in a separate bowl and pour over the aubergine (eggplant) mixture. Mix well and serve.

Sesame Seed Chutney

This chutney is particularly delicious served with Spiced Rice & Lentils (see page 49).

2.5 points

NUTRITIONAL INFORMATION

Calories	147	Protein	5g
Carbohydrate	1g	Sugars	0g
Fat	14g	Saturates	2g

🍲 10 MINS   🕐 5 MINS

SERVES 4

I N G R E D I E N T S

8 tbsp sesame seeds

2 tbsp water

½ bunch fresh coriander (cilantro)

3 fresh green chillies, chopped

1 tsp salt

2 tsp lemon juice

chopped red chilli, to garnish

1 Place the sesame seeds in a large, heavy-based saucepan and dry roast.

2 Set the sesame seeds aside to cool.

3 Once cooled, place the sesame seeds in a food processor or pestle and mortar and grind to form a fine powder.

4 Add the water to the sesame seeds and mix together to form a smooth paste.

5 Using a sharp knife, finely chop the coriander (cilantro).

6 Add the chillies and coriander (cilantro) to the sesame seed paste and grind once again.

7 Add the salt and lemon juice to the mixture and grind once again.

8 Remove the mixture from the food processor or pestle and mortar. Transfer to a serving dish and garnish.

COOK'S TIP

Dry roasting coaxes all of the flavour out of dried spices and gives dishes well-harmonized flavours that do not taste raw. Dry roasting only takes a few minutes and you will be able to tell when the spices are ready because of the wonderful fragrance that develops. Be sure to stir the spices constantly and never take your eyes off the pan because the spices can burn very quickly.

Carrot Dessert

This makes a very impressive dinner-party dessert. It is best served warm, with fresh cream if desired, and can be made in advance as it freezes well.

NUTRITIONAL INFORMATION

Calories	817	Protein	12g
Carbohydrate	89g	Sugars	87g
Fat	48g	Saturates	23g

10 MINS   55 MINS

SERVES 4

I N G R E D I E N T S

1.5 kg/3 lb 5 oz carrots

10 tbsp ghee

600 ml/1 pint/2½ pints milk

175 ml/6 fl oz/¾ cup evaporated milk

10 whole cardamoms, peeled and crushed

8–10 tbsp sugar

T O D E C O R A T E

25 g/1 oz/¼ cup pistachio nuts, chopped

2 leaves varq (silver leaf) (optional)

1 Rinse, peel and grate the carrots.

2 Heat the ghee in a large, heavy saucepan.

3 Add the grated carrots to the ghee and stir-fry for 15–20 minutes or until the moisture from the carrots has evaporated and the carrots have darkened in colour.

4 Add the milk, evaporated milk, cardamoms and sugar to the carrot mixture and continue to stir-fry for a further 30–35 minutes, until it is a rich brownish-red colour.

5 Transfer the mixture to a large shallow dish.

6 Decorate with the pistachio nuts and varq (if using) and serve at once.

COOK'S TIP

I like to use pure ghee for this dessert as it is rather special and tastes better. However, if you are trying to limit your fat intake, use vegetable ghee instead.

Pistachio Dessert

Rather an attractive-looking dessert, especially when decorated with varq, this is another dish that can be prepared in advance.

14 points

NUTRITIONAL INFORMATION

Calories	802	Protein	20g
Carbohydrate	99g	Sugars	98g
Fat	39g	Saturates	10g

 15 MINS 25 MINS

SERVES 6

I N G R E D I E N T S

850 ml/1½ pints/3½ cups water

250 g/9 oz/3 cups pistachio nuts

250 g/9 oz/1¾ cups full–cream dried milk

450 g/1 lb/2⅓ cups sugar

2 cardamoms, with seeds crushed

2 tbsp rosewater

a few strands saffron

T O   D E C O R A T E

25 g/1 oz flaked almonds

fresh mint leaves

1 Boil about 1 pint/600 ml water in a saucepan. Remove the pan from the heat and soak the pistachios in this water for about 5 minutes. Drain and remove the skins.

2 Grind the pistachios in a food processor or pestle and mortar.

3 Add the dried milk powder to the ground pistachios and mix well.

4 To make the syrup, place the remaining 300 ml/½ pint water and the sugar in a pan and heat gently. When the liquid begins to thicken, add the cardamom seeds, rosewater and saffron.

5 Add the syrup to the pistachio mixture and cook for about 5 minutes, stirring, until the mixture thickens. Set the mixture aside and leave to cool slightly.

6 Once cooled enough to handle, roll the mixture into balls (use up all of the pistachio mixture). Decorate with the flaked almonds and fresh mint leaves and leave to set before serving.

COOK'S TIP

It is best to buy whole pistachio nuts and grind them yourself, rather than using packets of ready-ground nuts. Freshly ground nuts have the best flavour as grinding releases their natural oils.

Almond Slices

A mouth-watering dessert that is sure to impress your guests, especially if served with whipped cream

10.5 points

NUTRITIONAL INFORMATION

Calories 531   Protein 8g
Carbohydrate ... 69g   Sugars 11g
Fat .... 27g   Saturates 11g

10 MINS   50 MINS

SERVES 6

INGREDIENTS

3 medium eggs

75 g/2¾ oz/½ cup ground almonds

200 g/7 oz/1½ cups milk powder

200 g/7 oz/1 cup sugar

½ tsp saffron strands

100 g/3½ oz/8 tbsp unsalted butter

25 g/1 oz/1 tbsp flaked almonds

1 Beat the eggs together in a bowl and set aside.

2 Place the ground almonds, milk powder, sugar and saffron in a large mixing bowl and stir to mix well.

3 Melt the butter in a small saucepan.

4 Pour the melted butter over the dry ingredients and mix well with a fork.

5 Add the reserved beaten eggs to the almond mixture and stir to blend well.

6 Spread the mixture in a shallow 15–20 cm/ 7–9 inch ovenproof dish and bake in a pre-heated oven at 160°C/325°F/Gas Mark 3 for 45 minutes. Test whether the cake is cooked through by piercing with the tip of a knife or a skewer – it will come out clean if it is cooked thoroughly.

7 Once it had cooled, cut the almond cake into even slices.

8 Decorate the almond slices with flaked almonds and transfer them to serving plates. Serve hot or cold.

COOK'S TIP

These almond slices are best eaten hot but they may also be served cold. They can be made a day or even a week in advance and re-heated. They also freeze beautifully.

Sweet Potato Dessert

This milky dessert can be eaten hot or cold.

4 points

NUTRITIONAL INFORMATION

Calories	254	Protein	5g
Carbohydrate	55g	Sugars	35g
Fat	3g	Saturates	1g

10 MINS   20 MINS

SERVES 8

INGREDIENTS

1 kg/2 lb 4 oz sweet potatoes

850 ml/1½ pints/3½ cups milk

175 g/6 oz/1¾ cups sugar

a few chopped almonds, to decorate

1 Using a sharp knife, peel the sweet potatoes. Rinse the sweet potatoes and cut them into slices.

2 Place the sweet potato slices in a large saucepan. Cover with 600 ml/1 pint/2½ cups milk and cook slowly until the sweet potato is soft enough to be mashed.

3 Remove the sweet potatoes from the heat and mash thoroughly to remove all the lumps.

COOK'S TIP

Sweet potatoes are longer than ordinary potatoes and have a pinkish or yellowish skin with yellow or white flesh. As their name suggests, they taste slightly sweet.

4 Add the sugar and the remaining 300 ml/½ pint/1¼ cups milk to the mashed sweet potatoes, and carefully stir to blend together.

5 Return the pan to the heat and leave the mixture to simmer until it starts to thicken (it should reach the consistency of a cream of chicken soup).

6 Transfer the sweet potato dessert to a serving dish.

7 Decorate the sweet potato dessert with the chopped almonds. Serve warm.

Sweet Saffron Rice

This is a traditional dessert which is quick and easy to make and looks very impressive, decorated with pistachio nuts and varq (silver leaf).

7.5 points

NUTRITIONAL INFORMATION

Calories 462	Protein 4g	
Carbohydrate ... 97g	Sugars 57g	
Fat 8g	Saturates 4g	

15 MINS   25 MINS

SERVES 4

INGREDIENTS

200 g/7 oz/1 cup basmati rice

200 g/7 oz/1 cup sugar

1 pinch saffron strands

300 ml/½ pint/1¼ cups water

2 tbsp ghee

3 cloves

3 cardamoms

25 g/1 oz/2 tbsp sultanas

TO DECORATE

a few pistachio nuts (optional)

varq (silver leaf) (optional)

1 Rinse the rice twice and bring to the boil in a saucepan of water, stirring. Remove the pan from the heat when the rice is half-cooked, drain the rice and set aside.

2 In a separate saucepan, boil the sugar and saffron in the water, stirring, until the syrup thickens. Set aside.

3 In another saucepan, heat the ghee, cloves and cardamoms, stirring occasionally. Remove the pan from the heat.

4 Return the rice to a low heat and add the sultanas, stirring well to combine.

5 Pour the syrup over the rice mixture and stir.

6 Pour the ghee mixture over the rice and leave to simmer over a low heat for 10–15 minutes. Check to see whether the rice is cooked; if not, add a little water, cover and leave to simmer gently.

7 Serve warm, decorated with pistachio nuts and varq (silver leaf), and with cream if desired.

COOK'S TIP

For a slightly stronger saffron flavour, place the saffron strands on a small piece of kitchen foil and toast them lightly under a hot grill (broiler) for a few moments (take care not to overcook them or the flavour will spoil) and crush finely between your fingers before adding to the sugar and water in step 2.

Almond & Pistachio Dessert

Rich and mouth-watering, this dessert can be prepared in advance of the meal. It is best served cold.

15 points

NUTRITIONAL INFORMATION

Calories 757	Protein 13g	
Carbohydrate ... 58g	Sugars 56g	
Fat 54g	Saturates 17g	

10 MINS　　20 MINS

SERVES 4

I N G R E D I E N T S

75 g/2¾ oz/6 tbsp unsalted butter

200 g/7 oz/1 cup ground almonds

200 g/7 oz/1 cup sugar

150 ml/5 fl oz/⅔ cup single (light) cream

8 almonds, chopped

10 pistachio nuts, chopped

1 Place the butter in a medium-sized saucepan, preferably non-stick. Melt the butter, stirring well.

2 Gradually add the ground almonds, cream and sugar to the melted butter in the pan, stirring to combine. Reduce the heat stir the mixture constantly for 10–12 minutes, scraping the bottom of the pan.

COOK'S TIP

This almond dessert can be made in advance and stored in an airtight container in the refrigerator for several days.

3 Increase the heat until the mixture turns a little darker in colour.

4 Transfer the almond mixture to a shallow serving dish and smooth the top with the back of a spoon.

5 Decorate the top of the dessert with the chopped almonds and pistachios.

6 Leave the dessert to set for about 1 hour, then cut into diamond shapes and serve cold.

Rice Pudding

Indian rice pudding is cooked in a saucepan over a low heat rather than in the oven like the British version – which is also far less sweet.

3 points

NUTRITIONAL INFORMATION

Calories 181	Protein 6g
Carbohydrate . . . 36g	Sugars 29g
Fat 2g	Saturates 2g

10 MINS   35 MINS

SERVES 8

I N G R E D I E N T S

75 g/2¾ oz/¼ cup basmati rice

1.2 litres/2 pints/5 cups milk

8 tbsp sugar

varq (silver leaf) or chopped pistachio nuts, to decorate

1 Rinse the rice and place in a saucepan. Add 1 pint/ 600 ml/ 2½ cups milk and bring to the boil over a very low heat. Cook until the milk has been completely absorbed by the rice, stirring occasionally.

2 Remove the pan from the heat. Mash the rice, making swift, round movements in the pan, for at least 5 minutes until all of the lumps have been removed.

3 Return the pan to the heat and gradually add the remaining 1 pint/ 600 ml/2½ cups milk. Bring to the boil over a low heat, stirring occasionally.

4 Add the sugar and continue to cook, stirring constantly, for 7–10 minutes or until the mixture is quite thick in consistency.

5 Transfer the rice pudding to a heatproof serving bowl. Decorate with varq (silver leaf) or chopped pistachio nuts and serve on its own.

COOK'S TIP

Varq is edible silver used to decorate dishes for special occasions. It is silver, beaten until it is wafer thin, and comes with a piece of backing paper which is peeled off as it is laid on the cooked food. It must be handled with great care. You can buy varq in Indian food stores, and because it is pure silver it should be stored in an airtight bag or box so that it does not tarnish.

Coconut Sweet

Quick and easy to make, this sweet is very similar to coconut ice. Pink food colouring may be added towards the end if desired.

NUTRITIONAL INFORMATION

Calories	586	Protein	7g
Carbohydrate	27g	Sugars	27g
Fat	51g	Saturates	40g

 10 MINS   15 MINS

SERVES 4

INGREDIENTS

75 g/2¾ oz/6 tbsp butter

200 g/7 oz/3 cups desiccated (shredded) coconut

175 ml/6 fl oz/¾ cup condensed milk

a few drops of pink food colouring (optional)

1 Place the butter in a heavy-based saucepan and melt over a low heat, stirring so that the butter doesn't burn on the bottom of the pan.

2 Add the desiccated (shredded) coconut to the melted butter, stirring.

3 Stir in the condensed milk and the pink food colouring (if using) and mix continuously for 7–10 minutes.

4 Remove the saucepan from the heat, set aside and leave the coconut mixture to cool slightly.

5 Once cool enough to handle, shape the coconut mixture into long blocks and cut into equal-sized rectangles. Leave the sweet to set for about 1 hour, then serve.

COOK'S TIP

Coconut is used extensively in Indian cooking to add flavour and creaminess to various dishes. The best flavour comes from freshly grated coconut, although ready-prepared desiccated (shredded) coconut, as used here, makes an excellent stand-by. Freshly grated coconut freezes successfully, so it is well worth preparing when you have the time.

Indian Vermicelli Pudding

Indian vermicelli (seviyan), which is very fine, is delicious cooked in milk and ghee. Muslims make this for Eid, which is celebrated at the end of Ramadan.

12.5 points

NUTRITIONAL INFORMATION

Calories 669	Protein 15g
Carbohydrate ... 84g	Sugars 77g
Fat 33g	Saturates 11g

3 HRS 10 MINS   20 MINS

SERVES 4

INGREDIENTS

25 g/1 oz pistachio nuts (optional)

25 g/1 oz flaked almonds

3 tbsp ghee

100 g/3½ oz/1½ cups seviyan (Indian vermicelli)

850 ml/1½ pints/3½ cups milk

175 ml/6 fl oz/¾ cup evaporated milk

8 tbsp sugar

6 dates, stoned and dried

1 Soak the pistachio nuts (if using) in a bowl of water for at least 3 hours. Peel the pistachios and mix them with the flaked almonds. Chop the nuts finely and set aside.

2 Melt the ghee in a large saucepan and lightly fry the seviyan (Indian vermicelli). Reduce the heat immediately (the seviyan will turn golden brown very quickly so be careful not to burn it), and if necessary remove the pan from the heat (do not worry if some bits are a little darker than others).

3 Add the milk to the seviyan (Indian vermicelli) and bring to the boil slowly, taking care that it does not boil over.

4 Add the evaporated milk, sugar and the stoned dates to the mixture in the pan. Leave to simmer for 10 minutes, uncovered, stirring occasionally. When the consistency starts to thicken, pour the pudding into a serving bowl.

5 Decorate the pudding with the chopped pistachio nuts and flaked almonds.

COOK'S TIP

You will find seviyan (Indian vermicelli) in Indian grocers. This dessert can be served warm or cold.

This is a Parragon Book
This edition published in 2002

Parragon
Queen Street House
4 Queen Street
Bath BA1 1HE, UK

ISBN: 0-75257-722-0

Printed in China

NOTE

This book uses metric and imperial measurements. Follow the same units of
measurement throughout; do not mix metric and imperial. All spoon measurements
are level: teaspoons are assumed to be 5 m, and tablespoons are assumed to be 15 ml.
Unless otherwise stated, milk is assumed to be full fat, eggs and individual vegetables
such as potatoes are medium and pepper is freshly ground black pepper.

The nutritional information provided for each recipe is per serving or per person.
Optional ingredients, variations or serving suggestions have not been included in the
calculations. The times given for each recipe are an approximate guide only because
the preparation times may differ according to the techniques used by different
people and the cooking times may vary as a result of the type of oven used.

Recipes using raw or very lightly cooked eggs should be
avoided by infants, the elderly, pregnant women, convalescents
and anyone suffering from an illness.